Discovery Walks
in
NORTH-EAST DERBYSHIRE

Elaine Burkinshaw

Published by Sigma Leisure – an imprint of
Sigma Press, 1 South Oak Lane, Wilmslow, Cheshire SK9 6AR, England.

British Library Cataloguing in Publication Data
A CIP record for this book is available from the British Library.

ISBN: 1-85058-740-X

Typesetting and Design by: Sigma Press, Wilmslow, Cheshire.
Cover Design: MFP Design and Print

Cover photographs: top, Holy Moor near Holymoorside; bottom, Ogston Reservoir in the Amber Valley *(North East Derbyshire District Council)*
Photographs within the book: Elaine Burkinshaw
Maps: Jeremy Semmens

Printed by: MFP Design and Print

Disclaimer: the information in this book is given in good faith and is believed to be correct at the time of publication. No responsibility is accepted by either the author or publisher for errors or omissions, or for any loss or injury howsoever caused. Only you can judge your own fitness, competence and experience.

Contents

Introduction

Early Man

Great Halls and Country Houses

Transport Links

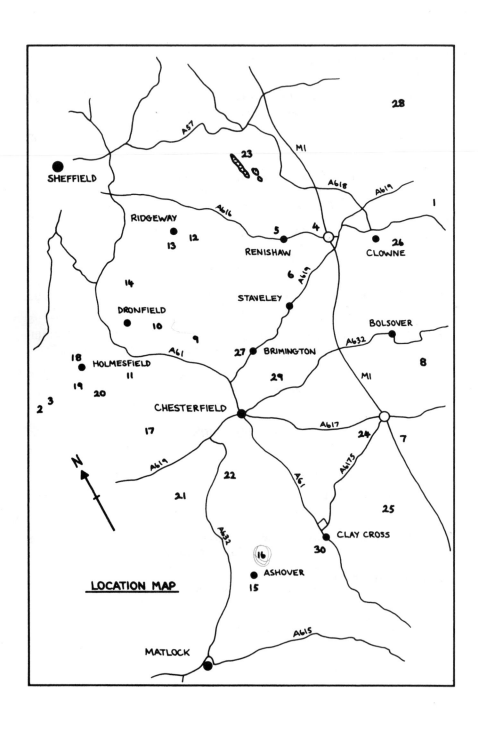

LOCATION MAP

Introduction

The county of Derbyshire is situated in the heart of England and is in the minds of most people automatically associated with the tourist thronged Peak District, however, in the North-East of the county, outside the National Park, lies an unspoilt and well kept secret. Derbyshire is the home of some of England's most stunning scenery and the North-East corner is no exception. This comparatively small area plays host to a diverse range of predominantly rural scenery, with extensive views. When combined with the architectural wealth and the memorials to man's industrial history, this creates a walker's paradise waiting to be unlocked in the panoramic valleys of the Amber, Cordwell, Drone, Hipper and Moss.

The busy market town of Chesterfield is central to this undiscovered area of a famous county set amidst outstanding natural beauty. To the north of the county lies South Yorkshire, Nottinghamshire is to the east and, as already mentioned the Peak District National Park sits over to the west. The whole of the region is easily accessible from the M1 and is close to the cities of Derby, Manchester, Nottingham and Sheffield.

About this guide

Within the boundaries of North-East Derbyshire lies an interesting mixture of scenery. A belt of magnesian limestone runs along the eastern edge. This has resulted, for example, in the gorge and caves at Creswell Crags. To the west of the limestone, the gently rolling landscape is a rapidly alternating blend of urban and rural scenery, which has developed as a result of its underlying coal measures and the growth of associated industrialisation during and after the Industrial Revolution. In the course of a century small-scattered agricultural communities had increased their population dramatically and become hives of industrial activity, only at a later stage to be reduced to economic ghost towns and villages as every pit was closed. On the western flank of North-East Derbyshire the landscape is much more akin, yet softer than the neighbouring Peak District. It is English green and pleasant countryside at its best. Gentle wooded valleys, fields, streams and farms punctuated by small, secluded stone built villages barely touched by the 20th century.

The history of the area has clearly been shaped by its wealth of natural resources, including iron, lead, limestone and coal. It is a region where towns and villages have evolved in tune with the land to serve those who work the land. The era of these traditional industries may now be over, but they leave few scars on the land, as sensitive environmental and conservation regeneration programmes are rapidly creating "new countryside", whilst at the same time preserving the local heritage.

The aftermath of coal mining does not conjure up glamorous or enticing images, therefore, it is important to stress at this stage that the rejuvenation process has very effectively camouflaged past activities, especially if you are prepared to get off the beaten track. Often it is only the rows of colliery houses in the towns and villages that remind you of the immense impact that coal mining had on this area. On the other hand, I believe that it should not be forgotten that North-East Derbyshire and its people were at the heart of industrial development that was to change the world and transform Britain into the first industrial nation.

It would appear that many other people share my view and take great pride in the legacy and contribution of earlier generations in creating the Mid-Victorian "workshop of the world" (Benjamin Disraeli 1858). There are numerous ongoing and planned local projects, often utilising the partnership approach for best results, which concentrate not only on restoring the landscape, but they have also taken on board the industrial theme in their heritage revival. To lose the heritage of North-East Derbyshire would be to lose its character. Thankfully, there is great public interest and support in salvaging and preserving the sites and products of the Industrial Revolution. Closed collieries, derelict railway lines and stagnant waterways are all being renovated to meet the enormous leisure and educational appetite of the local people and hopefully to tempt more visitors into the area.

The aim of this walking guide is to promote a less well-known and hence undervalued tourist area by transporting the walker back in time on a voyage of discovery and providing an insight into the local heritage. All the family can enjoy the walks, as they are all of modest length and are gentle circular trails offering education and relaxation away from the pressures of the modern world. The walks are all based on a theme and are arranged in rough chronological "chapters", which you can dip in to in any particular order along the history highway. Each "chapter" follows in the footsteps of past generations that all have their own fascinating story to tell. History brought alive and complimented by attractive scenery brings an extra dimension to walking. Immerse yourself in the spirit of the history, to see the invisible, touch the intangible and feel the experience.

Historical Overview

Abundant traces of Palaeolithic man have been found at Creswell Crags dating back to the Ice Age in the gorge and caves cut into the magnesian limestone by the subterranean erosion of water. These finds have placed the narrow ravine in the public spotlight and it is hoped in the coming years to capitalise on the importance of Creswell Crags with a substantial expansion of the site. Other Palaeolithic remains have also been found at the nearby Ash Tree Cave and at Whaley. More recent Iron Age remains have come to light in the Markland Grips, which again is a close neighbour of Creswell Crags. In addition, on the lonely and desolate Ramsley Moor on the edge of The Peak National Park, evidence of Neolithic man has been discovered.

In the middle of North-East Derbyshire lies the market town of Chesterfield, which makes it the natural touring centre for the region. Chesterfield, or Cestrefield, as it was known then, was a small Roman settlement at the confluence of the River Hipper and River Rother, which was of strategic importance as it lay in the path of vital trade routes to the north, south and west. The Romans initially set up camp here as they marched out of Derby and headed north along Ryknield Street, the modern day A61. Later they built a fort in Chesterfield and hence the name Cestrefeld, the open field below the fort.

Chesterfield was created a market town by Royal Charter in 1204 and this status has remained of great importance to the town. In 1598 Elizabeth I granted a second charter to Chesterfield, which marked the end of a long struggle with the sixth Earl of Shrewsbury, the Lord of the Manor, to establish the rights and privileges of the towns burgesses. Famous travellers passing through Chesterfield include in the 17th century Celia Fiennes, who commented "The town looks well, the Streets good, the Market very large". Later in the 18th century, Daniel Defoe noted "a very good market, well stored with provisions". Even today, the market remains one of the largest open-air markets in the country. Chesterfield prospered during medieval times as a town of guilds. However, two important developments thrust Chesterfield into the Industrial Revolution. First the building of the Chesterfield Canal and later the construction of the railways.

Chesterfield's most famous landmark is its crooked spire of the Parish Church of St Mary's and All Saints, which remains the symbol of Chesterfield and is a distinctive and "inspiring" memory of many of the views in this book. The church is the largest in Derbyshire and has an eight-sided 228ft wooden spire tiled in lead, which leans nine feet, four inches to the south west and three feet, two inches to the west. There has been a church on this site since the seventh century, however, the only remains of the original church is the font, which was found in the vicarage gardens in 1898. The present church dates back to Norman times, although the spire was not completed until the mid-fourteenth century.

The reason for the spire becoming twisted over the years has been lost in history and is the subject of many legends. The most likely explanation is that it would have been built at a time when many people including local skilled craftsmen lost their lives to the Black Death. Therefore, inexperienced workers may have used green, rather than seasoned timbers. The passage of time, the weight of 32 tons of lead and the effects of the weather have all contributed to the gradual leaning and distortion of the spire.

The growth of the landed gentry from the late sixteenth century onwards has left North-East Derbyshire with more than its fair share of distinguished and beautiful country houses. There is Barlborough Hall, Renishaw Hall (home of the Sitwell family), the Old and New Halls at Hardwick (built by the famous Bess of Hardwick), Bolsover Castle (built by the son and grandson of Bess of Hardwick) and Sutton Scarsdale Hall (connected with the Earl of Scarsdale).

The area can also boast an odd contribution to changing the course of history. At the Revolution House in Old Whittington, which was originally an ale house, local noblemen met to conspire to overthrow James II and replace him with William of Orange and James's daughter Mary in the Glorious Revolution of 1688.

Minerals have been mined in the area for centuries dating back to pre-Roman "industrialists", but on a comparatively small scale and in shallow mines. Thus, although the areas links with coal mining go back deeper into the past than might be expected, it was only from the mid-19th century that the intensive exploitation of coal began, as one of the basic and traditional industries. Numerous deep shafts were sunk, which have laid the foundations for rich seams of history.

This increasing importance of coal mining in "modern times" greatly multiplied the output of coal in the area and came essentially as the result of a better transport system. Coal mining on a large scale required a reliable means of moving its bulk cargoes to its markets. The Chesterfield Canal, surveyed by James Brindley and completed by 1777, was first on the scene and linked the town of Chesterfield with the River Trent. As one of the early generation of canals, it heralded a huge step forward for its time. It was the golden age of steam railways, however, that provided the main impetus and allowed the local collieries to compete with the coal fields in the North-East of England and forge their way into the Industrial Revolution.

George Stephenson, the famous railway pioneer and his son Robert, both of whom are best known for their locomotive called "Rocket", were responsible for bringing the railways to North-East Derbyshire. George came to the area in search of a route for trains to run between Derby and Leeds. In 1837 he started work on the North Midland line and by chance whilst a tunnel was being dug under Clay Cross substantial coal reserves were discovered. The importance of Stephenson's two contributions to the area cannot be overstated. The combination of his railway line and his exploitation of the Clay Cross coal seams meant that by 1870 the collieries of Clay Cross were supplying one tenth of the coal entering London by rail and half of London's coal carried by rail came from Derbyshire.

The heyday for the coal barons of North-East Derbyshire when coal prices boomed was between the coming of the railways and the 1870s. The competition, however, became cut-throat and a price war ensued. This ended abruptly in 1873 with an agreement to work to a sensible pricing strategy. General economic problems in the last quarter of the 19th century set the scene for reduced working hours and bankruptcies. Improved mining techniques were also slow to reach North-East Derbyshire, which was another factor contributing to the slow decline of the industry. The last North-East Derbyshire pit was closed at Renishaw in 1989.

Abundant coal reserves and the transport system were two of the ingredients that aided North-East Derbyshire's industrial progress and prosperity. The other main fuel of the Industrial Revolution was that the coal measures also provided a source of iron ore. Therefore, the development of the coal and iron industry is closely inter-related. The iron industry had, however, begun to develop rapidly in the 17th century. The Earl of Shrewsbury had brought Flemish refugees in the late sixteenth century to Eckington, who were sickle makers and this led to the Moss Valley becoming an important area for the sickle and scythe industry. The Foljambes of Dronfield also had substantial iron mills for the time on their estate. Then, in the second half of the 17th century came the Sitwell iron-master dynasty that resided at Renishaw Hall.

From 1836 the iron industry expanded dramatically alongside coal and was assisted by the introduction of the hot air method of smelting, which reduced fuel consumption. By the 1870s, however, local ore could no longer meet the demands of the industry and it had to be imported. The decline of the industry then began, as in general Derbyshire produced low quality pig iron and was unable to keep up with technological advances, which started to end the life of the smaller businesses. The scene was to become dominated by two giant iron smelting businesses; The Sheepbridge Coal & Iron Company and The Staveley Coal & Iron Company Ltd. The former was shutdown in 1970 and the latter in 1930. The industry became uncompetitive and diversified into other engineering areas.

The towns based on the North-East Derbyshire coal fields suffered a similar fate. They have endured the stresses and strains of high unemployment, which has now been alleviated to a certain extent by the development of light industrial estates in their place.

Designated Walking Trails

This book utilises sections of the following trails:

* **The Trans Pennine Trail** – This national trail is currently under construction and will eventually provide a unique route for walkers and cyclists. From Chesterfield the trail already runs along the towpath of the Chesterfield Canal to Staveley. This 8-kilometre stretch alternates between quiet rural scenery, especially around Bluebank, to the powerful industrial landscape of Staveley.

* **The Beighton/Staveley Trail** – At Staveley the Trans-Pennine Trail follows the existing Beighton/Staveley Trail, part of the former Great Central Railways line, through Renishaw, Killamarsh and Beighton. Access into Rother Valley Country Park is available.

* **The Five Pits Trail** – This trail winds along the former mineral lines which served five large deep collieries at Tibshelf, Pilsley, Holmewood, Williamthorpe and Grassmoor. The scenery is a mixture of pleasant rolling countryside and more obvious areas of past industrial activity, which will become more established in the coming years with the help of local groups.

* **The South Chesterfield Way** – This is a 9 mile linear route passing through urban and rural landscapes linking Chesterfield to Clay Cross over varied terrain.

The Three Valleys Tourism Project

Much of the area covered by this book overlaps with the Three Valleys Tourism Project. This project has its base at the Tapton Lock Visitor

Centre on the Chesterfield Canal and has been established to promote environmentally friendly tourism in the three valleys of the Rivers Moss, Rother and Drone. The work of the local volunteers can already be seen on many of the walks in this book.

How to use this guide

All the walks in this books are based on historical themes. Whilst the walks may be completed in any order, the grouping enables you to journey through time. A local history guide precedes each theme and the basic route instructions then follow. A sketch map of the route is also included purely for illustration. For navigational purposes it is recommended that you use the appropriate 1: 25,000 Ordnance Survey Explorer map on a suitable scale of four centimetres to one kilometre.

Wherever possible, the walks in this book follow legal public rights of way. Rights of way are the single most important means by which we can enjoy the countryside and preserve it for future generations. Briefly, these comprise public footpaths (foot only), bridleways (on foot, horseback and pedal cycles) and byways (usually old roads used as public footpaths, for example, greenlanes). If you find your right of way obstructed, you should report the details to the appropriate County Council. Walkers usually have free access to canal towpaths and country parks and also to land owned, for instance, by the Forestry Commission or the National Trust. However, if you are in any doubt please always check with the owner. On occasions, permissive or concessionary footpaths have been used. These paths are shown on maps, but there is no legal right to use them and, therefore, they may be extinguished at any time.

Please respect ancient sites and remember to observe the Countryside Code:

* Guard against all fires
* Fasten all gates
* Keep dogs under proper control
* Keep to paths across farmland
* Avoid damaging fences, hedges and walls
* Leave no litter
* Safeguard water supplies
* Protect wildlife, wild plants and trees
* Go carefully on country roads
* Respect the life of the country

Early Man

Creswell Crags

Creswell Crags is a dramatic limestone gorge honeycombed with caves, which bisects the Nottinghamshire/North-East Derbyshire border. The animal and plant remains found in the caves provide a unique time capsule and tell the fascinating story of the origins of human life during the last Ice Age between 45,000 to 10,000 years ago. At that time, the caves were one of the most northerly places on Earth to have been inhabited by our ancient ancestors.

Following the discovery of human remains by archaeologists in the late 19th century, this miniature Cheddar Gorge has become one of Europe's most important sites for palaeontology and archaeology, which ranks alongside Stonehenge and Hadrian's Wall, although from the public perspective it is not as well known. Creswell Crags currently houses a visitor centre, which provides an interpretation and appreciation of the importance of the ravine in the evolution of man through interactive exhibits.

The entire gorge is already a scheduled ancient monument and a Site of Special Scientific Interest, however, from the first Victorian archaeologists the Crags have suffered from poor and inappropriate management, which have prevented the gorge from becoming a major tourist attraction. For example, early excavations were carried out in the caves by blasting them with dynamite and an unsuitable road and sewage works have been built in the gorge.

There are, however, now plans for substantial development in the gorge and the surrounding area under the impetus of a project called The Creswell Initiative. The heritage lottery fund is to provide the resources to implement the higher standards of management, conservation, infrastructure and interpretation that the site deserves to repair the damage done in the last century. More detail on the extensive and ambitious plans of The Creswell Initiative is on clear display in the visitor centre.

Ramsley Moor

The lonely and desolate Ramsley Moor and Big Moor were once the home of Neolithic man. Numerous barrows and several stone circles can be seen in the area.

Trail 1 – Creswell Crags

Distance: 11.3 kilometres/7 miles

Start: Creswell Crags Visitor Centre

Map: OS Explorer Sherwood Forest 28 (270)

Refreshments: Limited selection at the Visitor Centre and public houses in Whitwell

Toilets: Visitor Centre

Key Features: Creswell Crags and the village of Whitwell

In addition to Creswell Crags, the walk includes Whitwell – a village with a rich history and an attractive mix of old and more modern buildings.

Route Instructions

1. From the car park, walk past the visitor centre and take the path immediately off to the left, sign posted "To the Crags". This path leads up to the Crags Pond. There is a track down each side of the pond and either option may be taken. At the end of the pond, head for a gate over to the right and onto the B6042.

2. Turn left and then right at the T-junction onto the A616 into Creswell. In 75 metres turn right at a public footpath sign and then in 50 metres climb a stile on the left, where a signpost advises "Whitwell 2 miles". Follow the path across a field to a stile on your right. Climb the stile and walk through the middle of a field to a line of trees. Inside the trees there is a path off to the left. Ignore the next stile on your left and instead climb the stile in front of you. Continue ahead in the same direction.

3. Just before reaching a railway line the path turns to the right in between two wire fences and leads up some steps. Turn left in front of some quarry workings, still walking in between two wire fences. The clear path follows a mound on your right and later bends around one end of the mound.

This hump was the 538-yard tunnel built in 1874 by the Midland Railway Company for the Mansfield to Worksop line.

The path then bends to the right at the other end of the mound. Turn left at a junction of paths and follow this track onto Sandy Lane, passing Bakestone Moor Old Post Office on the left.

4. At the crossroads, go straight across. The lane drops downhill, passing the Mallet and Chisel public house on the left and then bends to the right. At a T-junction, turn left onto Scotland Street. St Lawrence Church can now been seen at the T-junction ahead.

This is a twelfth-century Norman church with 14th and 15th century additions. Inside is the tomb of Sir Roger Manners (son of Sir John Manners and Dorothy Vernon of Haddon Hall in the Peak District).

Whitwell Hall is on Old Hall Lane at the side of the church. In 1592 the Old Hall was purchased by Sir John Manners, the son of the Earl of Rutland, from Elizabeth Hardwycke, a distant relation of Bess of Hardwick. The Manners family, as the Dukes of Rutland, continued to live at the hall until 1813 when the Duke of Portland purchased it. The hall has now been carefully restored and is a private dwelling, reached by turning left after St Lawrence Church onto Old Hall Lane. The hall is on the left-hand side. From an architectural point of view the hall is of great interest as it has an unusual floor plan and whilst the property is not open to the public, if you have a special interest in this type of premises the owners will by appointment provide a tour. The Victoria & Albert Museum in London has a painting of the hall called "Whitwell Hall, Church and Crags" dated 1785 by Samuel Grimm.

Turn right onto High Street

Manor House on High Street is one of the oldest buildings in the village. The Old George Inn, now flats, on High Street was once an 18th century coaching inn built on the Chesterfield to Worksop turnpike road. Lilac Cottage across from the George Inn was probably used as the Inn's stables. The Old Blacksmith's Shop on High Street has a wheelwright's stone built into the garden wall.

5. Walk down the hill to a junction with a memorial in the middle. Turn left by the memorial and head uphill. Take the first left onto Hangar Hill and then the first right onto Mill Lane leading to Mill Walk. At the end of the cul-de-sac there is a public footpath sign over to the right, which leads into a field. Head across the middle of the long field in the same direction making for a stile at the other side by a sign post, which allows you to cross over a railway line and climb another stile. Climb another stile in 20 metres. Follow a field edge with the hedge on your left to climb a stile. Now head for a stile in the far right-hand corner of the field ignoring all other stiles in this field. Cross the stile and turn left in 20 metres onto a track heading towards The Birks farmhouse.

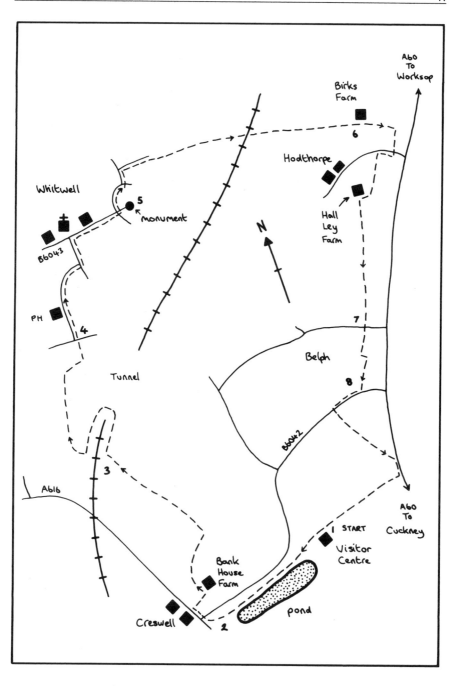

6. Look out for a stile on your right before the farmhouse. Cross this stile and then another one shortly afterwards to join a track. One hundred metres further on you climb a stile and turn right onto a track, which leads down to a lane. Turn right onto the lane and then left in 100 metres up the driveway to Hall Leys Farm. The lane bends to the right towards the farmhouse. At a signpost close to the farmhouse turn left to leave the lane and head across a field. Walk across three fields in total before reaching a lane at Belph.

7. Cross the lane and walk up the "No Through Road". At a T-junction of tracks turn left and pass Lilac Cottage on your left. At a public footpath sign, the track bends to the right and continues to a road.

8. Turn right onto the B6042 and after 250 metres, by a disused tip on your right, turn left onto a green lane, which is hedged on both sides. This lane leads to the A60. Turn right, and in 50 metres turn right again onto a track, which leads back to the visitor centre.

Trail 2 – Ramsley Moor: West ✓

Distance: 8 kilometres/5 miles
Start: Shillito Wood car park on Fox Lane off the B6051
Map: OS Outdoor Leisure 24 The Peak District White Peak Area
Refreshments: None
Toilets: None
Key Features: Ramsley Moor and Big Moor including a stone circle

Although the paths on this walk are all very clear, as with all moorland walks they should only be completed in good weather conditions. The paths are mainly concessionary and, therefore, their use can be withdrawn at any time.

Route Instructions

1. From the car park cross over Fox Lane and go through the gate opposite onto the Eastern Moors Estate. Drop downhill to a track. Ignore this first track, but turn right in 10 metres at the next junction. This clear track winds it way across Ramsley Moor and into Foxlane plantation. The weather-worn Ramsley Cross can be seen over to the right when you first join the track. Eventually the track leads through a gate onto Car Road. Continue straight ahead at this crossroad of tracks. The path gradually climbs uphill and round to the left to the A621. Smeekley Wood can be seen over to the right on first joining this path.

2. Cross over the A621 and pass through the white gate opposite onto a surfaced lane. On reaching a marker post bear left at the fork on the surfaced lane. Keep straight ahead at a crossroad of tracks. Just before a building close to Barbrook Reservoir turn left at a signpost for Barbrook Valley, which also warns you to beware of adders! This whole area is a developing wildlife sanctuary. Pass a small reservoir on your right and a stone circle on the left. The track leads to the A621.

This circle of 12 stones is one of the best preserved in Derbyshire, dating back to at least 1500 BC and they are all aligned to events such as Midsummer and Midwinter.

3. Cross over the road and pass through the gate opposite. Instead of continuing on the track immediately turn left on to an uphill path. Keep in the

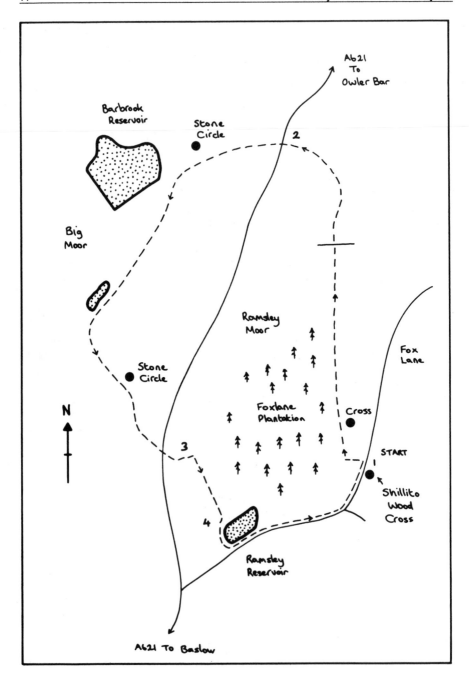

same direction for 75 metres to a grassy track at the top of the hill. Turn right, soon walking with Foxlane Plantation on the left and views of Ramsley Reservoir ahead.

4. By the reservoir turn right at a signpost to Fox Lane, walking with the reservoir on your left. At the corner of the reservoir turn left and walk along a bank top. Pass through a gate at the end of the reservoir and bear right over to Fox Lane. Turn left onto the lane and continue straight ahead at the T-junction. Shillito Wood and its stone cross are on the right. The lane returns to the car park on the right.

Trail 3 – Ramsley Moor: East ✓

Distance: 9 kilometres/5½ miles
Start: Shillito Wood car park, Fox Lane off the B6051
Map: OS Outdoor Leisure 24 The Peak District White Peak Area.
Refreshments: None
Toilets: None
Key Features: Ramsley Moor

Route Instructions

1. Turn left out of the car park onto Fox Lane. Walk past Shillito Wood on the left.

The Shillito Cross can be seen inside the wood. There are remains of bolehills in the area where lead smelting would have been carried out. Shillito Wood provided the necessary charcoal for this process.

At a T-junction turn right through a gate and join a clear track across Ramsley Moor. At a fork keep right.

The weather-worn Ramsley Cross can be seen to the right on the hillside.

The track leads into woodland and follows the route of a stream on the left. Eventually the track reaches some large stepping stones, which take you across the stream. One hundred metres further on go through a gate and onto a track.

2. Turn right to pass Smeekley Farm and then 75 metres further on turn left at a public footpath sign on to a path through Smeekley Wood. The path runs along a valley bottom with a stream on the left. Cross over the stream and continue straight ahead at a junction of paths by a public foot-path sign. The stream is now on the right. Leave the woodland by a stile next to a gate and continue in the same direction over a footbridge. Climb a stile in a wall onto the B6051. Take the second right, which is sign posted for Unthank.

3. Turn right in 30 metres over a stile by a public footpath sign. In 20 metres climb another stile and follow a grassy path, which bends to the left uphill. At the top of the hill pass through a gap in a hedge on the right, to follow a field edge with the hedge on the left. In the next field the hedge becomes

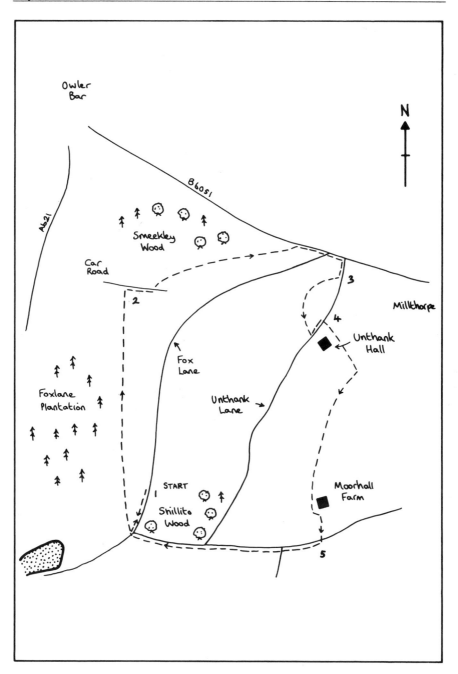

a wall. Keep to the field edge until reaching Unthank Lane by Unthank Hall. Turn left and follow the lane around a bend. Shortly after the bend there is a public footpath sign on the right.

4. Climb a stile into a field and walk across the middle of the field, passing farm buildings on the left, to a stile by a gate. Walk along a field edge with the hedge on the left and pass through a gate. Keep straight ahead in the next field, making for an entrance into Meekfield Wood. Immediately on entering the wood turn right and keep left at the fork in 20 metres. At the next fork, bear left again and follow the path across the wood over two streams and then head steeply uphill to emerge from the wood by a gate.

Go through the gate into a field and in 40 metres look out for a yellow waymarker on a tree that takes you back across the stream. Head uphill to a marker post and continue to a stile next to the buildings of Moorhall Farm. Walk with the barn on the left and just after the end of this building, climb a stile on the left to join the driveway to the farm. Turn right and walk to a lane.

5. Turn right onto the lane. Continue in the same direction, ignoring first a junction on the left and then one on the right, making towards a line of trees forming Shillito Wood. At the next T-junction turn right and retrace the lane back to the car park.

Great Halls and Country Houses

Barlborough Hall

Barlborough Hall lies just to the north of the village of Barlborough and was built in 1584 by Sir Francis Rodes with the assistance of the architect Robert Smythson, who is celebrated for his work at Hardwick Hall and Bolsover Castle. Sir Francis Rodes claim to fame is probably that he was one of the judges at the trial of Mary Queen of Scots. The Hall, a compact Elizabethan mansion, is now a preparatory school for Mount St Mary's College at Spinkhill and it is not open to the public except for a few days each year.

The Hall should not be confused with Barlborough Old Hall, which is actually the younger of the two properties and was built in 1618 by Robert Smthson's son John. The Old Hall, which is now a private house, is situated near the village centre, but if you have a special interest in the work of the Smythson architectural dynasty, viewing can be arranged by appointment only.

The Sitwell dynasty and Renishaw Hall

Renishaw Hall has been the ancestral home of the Sitwell family since 1625. However, it was not until the 20th century that Renishaw was immortalised by the prose and poetry of the three children, Edith, Osbert and Sacheverell, the offspring of the eccentric Sir George Sitwell and his wife, Lady Ida Sitwell.

Traces of the Sitwells, or the Sytwells, can be found as far back as the early 14th century at the nearby village of Ridgeway. Robert Sytwell from Staveley acquired the site of the present park around 1540, although he did not actually undertake any construction work. Robert was, however, a wealthy man, who had a lease on a coalmine at Eckington. Indeed, the Sitwell's made their fortune exploiting local coal and iron long before the Industrial Revolution, although they did not participate in the Industrial Revolution itself for reasons later outlined.

Robert died in 1599 leaving many of his properties to his Catholic wife. His heir, however, was his elderly Protestant cousin, who died shortly after a long legal battle to acquire Robert's Eckington estates. In 1600, George Sitwell the grandson of the heir to Robert's fortune was born and he was the first to build at Renishaw. His H-shaped small manor house forms the nucleus of the present house.

George moved into the house with his bride in 1625. He defended

Renishaw for the King during the Civil War and received frequent heavy fines from Cromwell. Fortunately, however, due to the extraordinary success of his local ironworks, George's finances were left intact despite Cromwell's efforts. By the end of the 17th century, the Sitwells' ironworks were producing one tenth of the output of nails in England.

George's son, Francis, was his successor, but he died only four years later. His widow, Katherine Sacheverell, was the sister of William Sacheverell, who created the Whig Party. William was guardian to his nephew George who succeeded to Renishaw at the age of ten.

The consecutive Sitwell owners of Renishaw through to the end of the 18th century were all Whigs and they all continued to amass great family fortunes and became well known in the City of London. However, the later generations of the Sitwells led extravagant lifestyles and suffered a string of financial disasters, which contributed to their downfall to the extent that in 1848 the estate and much of its contents had to be sold.

The discovery of large coal reserves close to the estate boundaries at a later stage went some way towards restoring the family wealth. However, despite the nearby Chesterfield Canal and later the railway, which provided ideal transport links, the Sitwells did not seize the opportunities presenting themselves in the same way as other Victorian industrialists, and the house lay largely empty and unlived in for much of the year.

Sir George Reresby Sitwell was born in 1860 and was to succeed as the fourth baronet at the age of two. His strict and eccentric way of life contrasted greatly with that of his outgoing and beautiful wife, Lady Ida, who was a niece of Wellington. It was the literary achievements of their three children that are most often associated with Renishaw. Indeed, all their siblings were clearly deeply affected by their upbringing, as they all have recorded their memories in their prose and poetry. In 1909, Sir George bought a castle in Tuscany to restore and eventually Sir George and Lady Ida were persuaded by their children to go and live there.

Renishaw then became the property and summerhouse of their eldest son Osbert. It was during the Second World War, that "Captain Osbert", as he was known by the locals, wrote his acclaimed five volume autobiography called "Left Hand, Right-hand", which recalls many of his fathers eccentricities and was illustrated by a famous series of paintings by John Piper.

In 1965, like his father, Osbert also had to give up Renishaw before his death, already having suffered with Parkinson's Disease for over a decade. Osbert handed the estate over to his nephew and grandson of Sir George Sitwell to Sir Reresby Sitwell, the seventh baronet. Sir Reresby and Lady Sitwell are the current owners of Renishaw Hall, although they spend much of their time at their London home. The hall is not open to the public except for organised groups by appointment, but a Sitwell museum, an art and costume gallery and craft workshops can be viewed in the Georgian stables.

The grounds are also open to the public and it is the eccentric Sir George Sitwell that we have to thank for creating 300 acres of beautiful formal Italian gardens adorned with pyramid hedges, fountains, statues, pools and lakes. There is also a vineyard in the park, which until fairly recently was the most northerly vineyard in Western Europe.

The village of Renishaw lies close to the hall and was the home of the family ironworks. The area later went on to become a large coal mining community. The Sitwell Arms built in 1850 served the Victorian railway traveller and has occasionally acted as a courthouse.

Hardwick Hall

In the late sixteenth century following the dissolution of the monasteries, a new Elizabethan landed class began to emerge, who built large grand mansions on their landscaped country estates. This was a time when there was a clear and competitive link between building and status. Building was on a scale for show, rather than function and a lofty position could elevate and advertise wealth and social position. The ultimate aim being to attract a royal visit with all its attendant opportunities and favours. Bess of Hardwick and Hardwick Hall provide us with a perfect example of this social structure. Indeed, probably no house in the country is so indelibly linked with one person and to find two large houses so close together produces a truly impressive effect.

Bess was the daughter of a Derbyshire squire, who owned a small manor house on the site of the Old Hall. She married four times, each time to a husband more wealthy and influential than the last. She outlived them all to become the richest and most powerful woman in England after Queen Elizabeth I. Bess was a formidable business woman, a builder of great houses, a collector and was highly ambitious both for herself on the marriage market and for her children. Her genetic engineering had important dynastic consequences as Bess and her second husband, William Cavendish, were the founders of the ducal families of Devonshire, Newcastle and Portland.

In 1543, Bess married her cousin Robert Barlow, who died a few months later. In 1547 she then married the elderly and wealthy Sir William Cavendish, which greatly enhanced her status. To please Bess he sold his considerable properties and bought new property in Derbyshire and Nottinghamshire, including the Chatsworth estate. The existing house was pulled down and a new one was built on the site of the present house. This was the only marriage that produced children for Bess.

William died in 1557, but two years later Bess was married again to William St Loe, who was from a better established family than the Cavendishes. He died five years later and her fourth and final marriage in 1567 to George Talbot, the sixth Earl of Shrewsbury, who was head of one of the oldest and richest families in England, was in property terms like the merging of two great companies.

Within two years of their marriage, Elizabeth I saddled George with the task of acting as custodian of Mary Queen of Scots through to 1584. Mary was moved between their many properties, but despite legend, she was never kept at Hardwick Hall.

In 1574, Bess took a great risk by secretly marrying her daughter Elizabeth to Charles Stuart, the brother of Mary Queen of Scots. Thus, on the death of the Queen any of their children would have a claim to the throne, which infuriated the Queen and upset George, who was a deeply patriotic man. From that time onwards her relationship with George became more and more strained. In 1575 the young married couple duly produced a child, Arabella Stewart. Both her parents died shortly afterwards and Bess found herself guardian to an extremely troublesome child, who became a pawn in the power game of politics and the monarchy, which eventually led to her tragic life coming to an end during imprisonment at the Tower of London.

Then in 1583 Bess bought the Hardwick property from her bankrupt brother. At this time Bess was still married, but separated from the Earl of Shrewsbury. Hardwick, rather than Chatsworth, became her principal home and initially she pooled her resources into rebuilding the manor house as the present Hardwick Old Hall. The death of the Earl in 1590, however, transformed her financial position and within a matter of weeks she commissioned Robert Smythson to design Hardwick Hall within metres of the Old Hall. Remains of the Old Hall still survive today in the hands of English Heritage.

Bess moved into the largely completed new hall in 1597. Standing on top of a windblown scarp, Hardwick Hall "more glass than wall", is one of the finest and most complete examples of Elizabethan architecture with an emphasis on symmetry that history and chance have miraculously preserved. Its majestic qualities led to it being regarded by contemporaries as a masterpiece of innovative features and ingenious design. Undoubtedly it was built to reflect the wealth and status of Bess, in the hope of a royal visit, or a Queen Arabella, although neither of these two dreams ever materialised. It has six imposing towers and the huge initials ES crowning the roofline. Unusually for the time the building was a storey higher than the norm and it also contained a vast area of windows and glass. Glass was an expensive material of the day and to use it on such a scale was another display of extravagance.

Hardwick survives today with many of its original contents as listed in an inventory taken in 1601. It has a unique antiquarian atmosphere and has escaped modernisation, without being left neglected, in the hands of the Cavendish family (the current Dukes of Devonshire) until 1959, when it was accepted in lieu of Death Duties and handed over to the National Trust.

Bolsover Castle

Bolsover Castle is an astonishing complex of sandstone buildings that stand dramatically on the top of a limestone ridge in the small market town of Bolsover dominating the landscape for miles around. Effectively two houses were built, one a dream romantic folly with lavish interior decoration and the other a terrace range for entertaining and accommodating important guests. Despite its commanding position it is, however, very much a castle in name only, as the remains are that of a mock medieval country house celebrating romance and chivalry, built on the site of a twelfth century castle. The sense of theatre created by this fantasy 17th century property contrasts strongly with the surrounding legacy of the industrial past of more recent centuries.

The mood of the castle has been encapsulated by many. In his masque "Loves Welcome To Bolsover", written for the visit of Charles I, Ben Johnson reminds us "This is not a warlike place, much of its imagery is intellectual, sensual and designed to evoke the virtues of romantic love". Sachevererell Sitwell from nearby Renishaw commented that Bolsover had "a ghostly poetry that fires the imagination, that can never be forgotton and that never cools".

The manor of Bolsover was given by William the Conqueror to William Peverel I. The Peverel family's other castle at Castleton was very similar. By the end of the 14th century the castle had fallen out of use, although it remained in Royal hands until 1553 when it was granted to Sir George Talbot, the sixth Earl of Shrewsbury and the fourth husband of Bess of Hardwick. Charles Cavendish, the youngest son of Bess by an earlier marriage, first leased and later bought the Bolsover estate from the seventh Earl of Shrewsbury. Charles, who inherited the building bug of his mother, also employed Robert Smythson the brilliant architect of Hardwick Hall to transform Bolsover, although both died before work had progressed very far.

The "Little Castle" which replaced the medieval keep constituted the first phase of building work. This was a richly decorated family suite within a self- contained keep, a Cavaliers' pleasure palace. Robert Smythson died in 1614 followed by Charles Cavendish in 1619. Their sons, John Smythson and William Cavendish continued with their fathers' scheme and incorporated their own ideas, which were influenced by the fashionable work of London's Inigo Jones.

In contrast to the "Little Castle", what would have been medieval defences along the ridge, were replaced by a terrace range of grand staterooms, which were later extended to cater for the visit of Charles I in 1634. The cost of the days banqueting entertainment was £15,000, which would equate to over £1,000,000 in today's terms.

John Smythson also designed a riding school for William, which was similar to William's other riding school at his nearby Welbeck Abbey property. The latter was one of the earliest riding schools. After John died in 1634, his son, Huntingdon, continued with the building work. Today it is one of the oldest surviving examples of its type in Europe.

William Cavendish was a well-known Royalist, a skilled horseman and a leading exponent on equitation. In 1665 he became the Duke of Newcastle and was nicknamed the Horsemanship Duke. During the civil war he commanded Royalist troops, but following defeat at Marston Moor in 1644 he was forced into exile. In Antwerp he established another riding school and published the famous Nouvelle Methode de Dresser les Chevaux in 1658 using views of Bolsover Castle as background to his illustrations.

Whilst William was in exile Bolsover Castle was captured and plundered by the Parliamentarians, but following the restoration of the monarchy in 1660 and William's return from exile the property had been returned to a habitable state by the time of his death in 1676.

By the 1740s Welbeck Abbey had become very much the principal residence of the heirs and Bolsover Castle was no longer occupied. From 1755 to 1945 the castle was in the hands of the Portland family, who transferred it to the nation. The castle is now looked after by English Heritage and it is without doubt a unique property.

The town of Bolsover was first granted a market charter in 1225. During the 18th century it was famous for its buckles and spurs and the manufacture of clay pipes. From the late-19th century, the town grew rapidly with the expanding coal mining industry. Indeed, the model village of New Bolsover built by the Bolsover Colliery Company is one of the finest and most important examples of colliery architecture in this country. It is of such great historical and architectural value that the entire village is listed.

Trail 4 – Barlborough Hall

Distance: 8 kilometres/5 miles

Start: Roadside parking on High Street, Barlborough in between the Rose & Crown and The Royal Oak

Map: OS Explorer 269 Chesterfield and Alfreton

Refreshments: Public Houses at Barlborough and Spinkhill

Toilets: None

Key Features: Barlborough Hall

Barlborough Hall is described in the introduction to this section.

Route Instructions

1. By the village hall turn onto Ruthyn Avenue and walk along the pavement on the right-hand side passing a primary school. The pavement leads onto a rough track called Ward Lane. Follow the lane up to the Hall on your right. At a junction of tracks at the Hall, continue straight ahead to a right-hand bend. At the bend leave the track and climb a stile in front of you to join a grassy track. The track moves ever closer to the M1 on your left. When you are opposite a bridge over the motorway, turn left at a marker post and cross over the bridge.

2. Turn right at the end of the bridge and then turn left in 50 metres at a junction of paths, to follow the edge of a field with a fence on your left. Climb a stile and continue in the same direction in the next field to the corner of a plantation. Climb another stile to now walk with one edge of the plantation on your right. Keep following the edge of the plantation to a field corner and then turn left. In the next field corner turn left and then, half way across the field, turn right to climb a stile. Walk along the right-hand edge of the field to a stile. After the stile, a track bends to the left to Parkhall Farm. At a T-junction of tracks turn right and follow the track to the road at Spinkhill.

3. Cross over the road and drop gently downhill, passing the Bootmakers Arms on your left and The Angel. At a right-hand bend, opposite a school, turn left onto a track. Keep straight ahead at a gate and follow the track downhill at first by a hedge on your right. After 100 metres, it bears left across the middle of a field. Cross a road and continue ahead, climbing

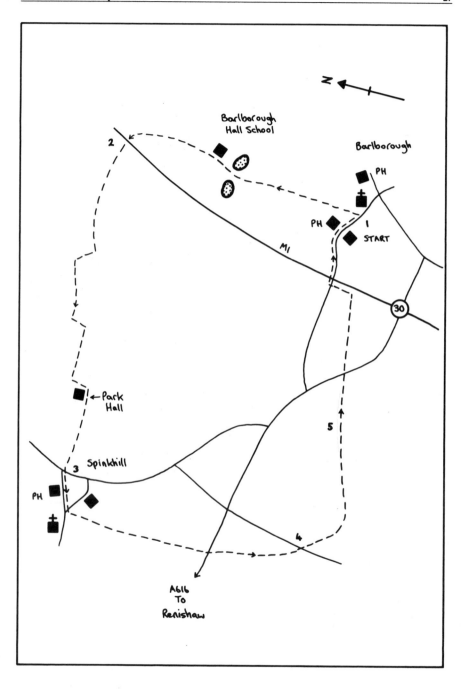

some steps to reach the A616. Turn left and then in 10 metres turn right onto a track. Just past a building the track becomes a path and follows a stream on your right. Keep left and then straight ahead at the following junction to a stile. Follow the path as it climbs uphill, passing through a gap in the hedge and then to a stile onto a lane.

4. Cross over the lane and take the path by the marker post opposite into woodland. At a fork, keep left and than ignore all side turnings until you emerge at the other end of the wood. The next stage may be a little tricky to navigate, as there is no clear path. On emerging from the very end of the wood, turn left to follow a field edge as it winds uphill to the field corner. Here pass through a gap in between two hedges and walk around the edge of the hedge on your right. On the other side of the hedge walk uphill for 50 metres and, before reaching the field corner, turn left to walk across the middle of a field heading for a gap in a line of trees with concrete posts in front of it. These trees mark the line of a dismantled railway line.

5. Pass in between the trees to join a grassy path, which is now visible on the ground and walk diagonally across a field to the corner. Turn right to join a much clearer grassy track and continue in the same direction until reaching a dual carriageway. Cross over the road with extreme care to join a rough track opposite. This track bends to the left to join a road on the outskirts of Barlborough. Turn right to cross back over the motorway and return to your starting point.

Barlborough

Application Submitted For Historic Canal Cottage

©Ashley Franklin

Derbyshire Wildlife Trust is delighted to announce that plans have been submitted for the much-loved Aqueduct Cottage on Cromford Canal.

The old lock keeper's cottage, circa 19th Century, has long stood in ruin since its heyday when it was a small family home in an idyllic location. But, since then its condition has rapidly declined and it currently sits as a well-known ruin at the entrance to the Trust's Lea Wood Nature Reserve.

But this month, working in partnership with James Boon Architects, the Trust submitted a planning application to repair and repurpose the cottage.

Alex Morley who is leading on the project for the Trust said, "It's all part of helping as many people as possible understand why Lea Wood and the wider Derwent Valley is so special. The work will remain true to the original façade of this well documented, and well-loved, piece of Cromford Canal's history.

"People will be welcomed inside this historic gem to learn why the building and its location are so distinct and then invited go on to discover the magic and beauty of Lea Wood and its wild surroundings. It will be a real highlight on the well-trodden Cromford Canal."

Derbyshire Wildlife Trust have had ownership of the cottage since 2012. The drive to repair the cottage stemmed from the Trust's National Lottery Heritage Funded DerwentWISE project which looks after natural, cultural and industrial heritage throughout the Lower Derwent Valley.

The Trust hope to hear whether or not plans have been successful in April 2019. To support the Trust with this work, become a member at www.derbyshirewildlifetrust.org.uk/join

ACCOUNTS:

Angela Green
angela@stoneleisure.com
Tel: 07908 706 177

WEBSITE:

RipleyAndAlfretonChronicle.com

PUBLISHED BY:

Stone Leisure Publishing Ltd

Belper Golden Rainbows Support Group

...held...
February...
on Cromford Road in the...

All money raised from the evening...
sales, donations and the raffle was do...
to Derbyshire Carers Association which is th...
chosen charity.

Councillor Lobley said, 'I was delighted to see so
many people attend this charity event to support
such an important and worthwhile organisation. The

Lo...
of Derbys...
£935.00 for the...

The Derbyshire LGBT + Project Officer Hate Crime Advocate - John Yates-Harold, (recent guest speaker at Belper Golden Rainbows support group) announced a general invitation to witness the official opening of the new Derbyshire LGBT + centre in Chesterfield at Rutland Road on March 1st.

In addition to the existing HQ at Bramble Street in Derby, this is a new hub to meet the increased need for LGBT + support in north Derbyshire where Chesterfield residents can access vital LGBT + services and view an excellent LGBT + History Exhibition.

The event was a great success well supported by the staff and volunteers who have worked hard since last August to make it all possible. We were presented

with a delicious array of free food, hot and cold drinks.

Toby Perkins MP and the Mayor of Chesterfield gave strong pro LGBT + speeches at the ribbon cutting ceremony.

Much gratitude to John who took the time and trouble to make us feel so special. He gave us a warm welcome together with a grand tour around the house enjoyed by my husband Terry and a few of friends who will benefit from visits to Rutland Ro...

info@derbyshirelgbt.org.uk

PHOTO: Grace Moronfolu MBE, Narvel Annable, Pet...
Terry Durand at the March 1st LGBT + event on Rutl...
Street.

Photograph was taken by John Yates-Harold

Trail 5 – Renishaw & Eckington

Distance: 9 kilometres/5½ miles

Start: Next to the Sitwell Arms at Renishaw on the A616. Heading towards the M1 the Sitwell Arms is on the left. The car parking area is not sign posted, but it is down a track immediately after the public house.

Map: OS Explorer 269 Chesterfield and Alfreton

Refreshments: The Sitwell Arms

Toilets: None

Key Features: A section of the Chesterfield Canal and a section of the Beighton-Staveley Trail (Trans Pennine Trail)

Route Instructions

1. From the car parking area there are three tracks in front of you. Take the track to the right. Ignore the two bridges side by side under the A616 and take a path off to the left. Keep ahead at a junction of paths in 30 metres and follow the line of the Chesterfield Canal passing Renishaw Foundry on your right. The path leads onto Spinkhill Lane. Here you leave the canal and turn right up the lane following the footpath on the left-hand side of the lane.

2. Just after a large sign for Mount St Mary's College at Spinkhill turn left onto a path on the colleges playing fields just before the church.

The college is built around Spinkhill and was once the home of the Pole family and later it became a public school run by Jesuits. Barlborough Hall is the preparatory school for the college. Joseph Hansom, who was the inventor of the Patent Safety Cab named after him, designed the church at Spinkhill.

The path follows the edge of the playing field so that you are walking back for a short while alongside the lane. In the field corner, turn right. On reaching a track, turn left. Here you leave the college grounds and head across the middle of a field.

3. 50 metres before some trees turn right at a T-junction. Follow the track as it bears to the right and then to the left. At a fork in the corner of the field leave the track and turn right onto a path, which runs alongside a stream and can be very muddy for about 20 metres. After following the edge of a field for a short distance turn right at a corner and head straight across

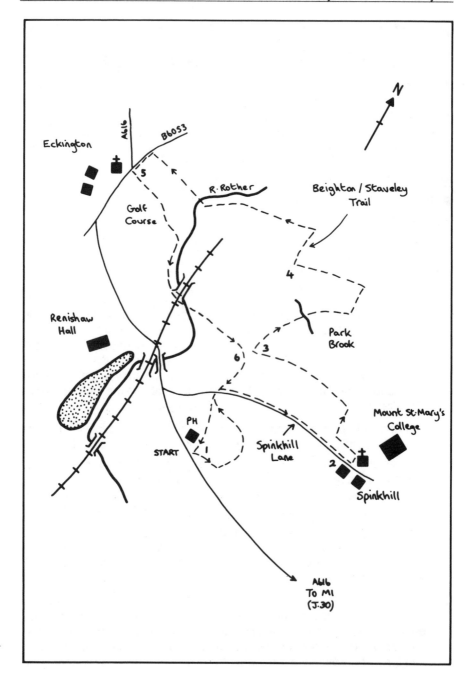

Eckington church

the middle of a field making for a metal post at the other side. After crossing the next field you arrive at a wide gravel track. Turn left onto this track and left again in 200 metres onto a lane. Just after crossing a bridge, bear right onto a downhill path by a marker post. Ignore all side tracks until you reach a T-junction with the Beighton — Staveley Trail, a former railway line.

4. Turn right onto the Trail and follow it for 200 metres to a crossroad of paths. Here turn left to leave the Trail and drop down some steps and over a stile. Follow the clear path in front of you across fields heading for a bridge over the River Rother. Cross a stile and walk under the bridge. The riverside path later bends to the right over a footbridge. Immediately after the footbridge, bear to the left to emerge onto a lane. Follow the lane to the B6053.

5. Turn left and in 50 metres climb a stile on the left. Walk straight ahead across the middle of a field to another stile. Climb the stile onto Renishaw golf course. Take care and respect the players whilst on the course. The route heads half right for 100 metres across a fairway making for a small marker post in some rough grass close to the end of a line of trees. Here a footbridge over the River Rother can be seen. Ignore this and follow a path to the right with the golf course on your right-hand side. Just before a green there is another small marker post, where you bear left to another footbridge over the river. Cross the footbridge and head half right to a stile. Climb the stile and keep ahead to some steps. The steps take you over a footbridge crossing a railway line. Turn right to head uphill. At the brow of the hill, walk straight ahead across a field to two stiles close together.

6. Climb the stile on the left and turn right onto a track, which initially follows a field edge and then begins to drop downhill. Ignore the first left and take the second left 100 metres further on to join a track with a fence on the right. At a T-junction in 30 metres turn right onto the Beighton – Staveley Trail. The Trail returns you to the car park.

Trail 6 – South from Renishaw

Distance: 6.5 kilometres/4 miles

Start: Next to the Sitwell Arms at Renishaw on the A616. Heading towards the M1 the Sitwell Arms is on the left. The car parking area is not sign posted, but it is down a track immediately after the public house.

Map: OS Explorer 269 Chesterfield and Alfreton

Refreshments: The Sitwell Arms

Toilets: None

Key Features: Sections of the Chesterfield Canal and the Beighton--Staveley Trail (Trans-Pennine Trail)

Route Instructions

1. From the car park there are three tracks in front of you. Take the track to the right. Ignore the bridge in front of you under the A616; take a path off to the left and then turn right in 10 metres to pass under another bridge with the traffic of the A616 above you, which joins the Chesterfield Canal towpath. Cross a footbridge over a stream to a lane.

2. Cross over and join the path opposite, which although it clearly follows the line of the canal there is no water and the path does become very overgrown during the summer months. For this reason, this is probably a walk best left for other times of the year when the route can be followed quite comfortably. At first, there is a wire fence on your right. As you continue across fields in the same direction you will pass a sewage works on your right and later you will walk with a hedge on your left. Cross over the track that leads to Huggester Farm on your left and now walk with the fence on your right.

3. At a fork continue straight ahead now walking along the top of an embankment. Drop down to a footbridge over the river Doe Lea and climb back up onto the embankment. The path leads over a large pipe and then, when you are faced with a fork near some more pipes, bear right to walk with the pipes on your left. On meeting a track turn right for five metres and right again. Pass through a gate in 75 metres and then at the fork immediately in front of you turn right up a hill. At a T-junction bear to the right to join the Beighton-Staveley Trail. The Trail leads back to a bridge, the former site of the Renishaw station, under the A616 at which point you retrace your steps to the car park.

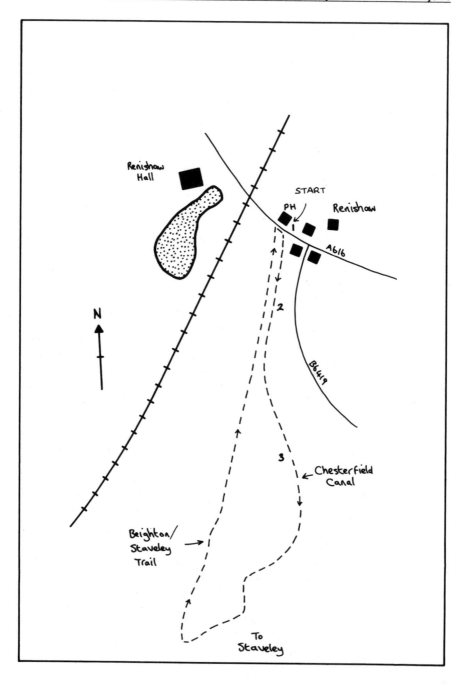

Trail 7 – Hardwick Hall

Distance: 13.5 kilometres/8½ miles

Start: Hardwick Country Park – Hardwick Ponds

Map: OS Explorer 269 Chesterfield and Alfreton

Refreshments: The Elm Tree Inn at Heath

Toilets: Hardwick Ponds car park

Key Features: Hardwick Hall, Hardwick Old Hall, Hardwick Ponds, Ault Hucknall Church, Stainsby Mill and the cottages of Heath

Route Instructions

1. Start from the information point/toilet block and take the path to the left around Miller Pond. Follow the path around the pond and shortly after passing through a second kissing gate turn left at a crossroad of paths.

2. When you see a gate and kissing gate in* front of you, look to the left for another kissing gate and go through it. Follow the gentle uphill path to another kissing gate in the top left-hand corner of the field.

3. Go through this gate, cross over the road, and continue ahead between trees. For the first 100 metres, a path cannot be seen on the ground, but if you keep roughly halfway between the road on the right and the fence on the left, a small marker post comes into view. A path then becomes visible and as you continue to climb it begins to swing to the left to a kissing gate in front of a cottage.

4. Follow the well-surfaced track to a lane.

Ault Hucknall church can be seen on the lane. This a small but interesting church, which has a black floor slab marking the burial place of the renowned 17th century political philosopher and author of 'The Leviation', Thomas Hobbes, who died at Hardwick Hall in 1679. Hobbes was tutor to the second and third Earls of Devonshire who resided at Hardwick. It also has a fine monument to the first Countess of Devonshire designed by John Smythson.

Turn left and follow Hodmire Lane passing one of the entrances to the Hardwick Estate on your left and then reaching Stainsby Mill on your right.

Stainsby mill is owned by the National Trust and excellently illustrates the workings of a nineteenth century water powered corn mill. A mill has actually stood on this site since the thirteenth century, first providing flour for the local villages and later for the Hardwick Estate. After years of neglect, the then owner of Hardwick Hall, the sixth Duke of Devonshire, restored it in 1850.

5. Continue past the mill to a T-junction. Here turn right and immediately cross over to a public footpath sign. Follow the direction of the sign up to a stile. Climb over the stile into a field and continue straight ahead with farm buildings on your right, to a stile not far away from the far right-hand corner of the field. After the stile, you drop down onto a lane.

6. Turn right and follow the lane past Stainsby Farm. At a left-hand bend, turn right onto a track sign posted for the Stainsby Centre. At the side of the Centre turn right and climb over a stile. At a wall corner, continue across a field and down past earthworks to a stile. Continue on and cross a footbridge over a stream. Follow the right-hand edge of the next field to a stile. Climb the stile and follow the edge of a field with wire fencing on your left to another stile. After the stile turn right on to a track. The track takes you over another stile before reaching the A6175.

7. Turn left and then shortly afterwards, turn right up a track by the side of a cottage. In 40 metres this joins a bend on the road through the charming village of Heath.

    The village has been designated a conservation area. Heath is recorded in the Domesday Book as two settlements. Lunt, on the site of the remains of the original twelfth century church. This is now separated from the village by the A617. Le Hethe was to the west. They probably combined into one village in the twelfth or thirteenth century. The village passed from Robert de Ferrars, the first Earl of Derby to the monks of Gerondon Abbey. After the Dissolution it passed, through several wealthy families. The village has two Grade II listed buildings, one being the remains of the church already mentioned and a thatched cottage at the northern end of the village.

8. Turn left at a public footpath sign just before the Old Reading Room cottage. Climb a stile into a field. Follow the left-hand edge of fields crossing two stiles to a lane. Turn left and then left again at the T-junction with the A6175. 100 metres after the petrol station turn right onto a track and follow this clear track ignoring all side turnings to Out Lane. Turn left and look out for a footpath that crosses the lane in several hundred metres.

9. Turn right over a stile into a field. Walk across the middle of the field to a stile. Follow the edge of the next field dropping downhill with the hedge on your right. In the field corner turn left, and then right over a stile fol-

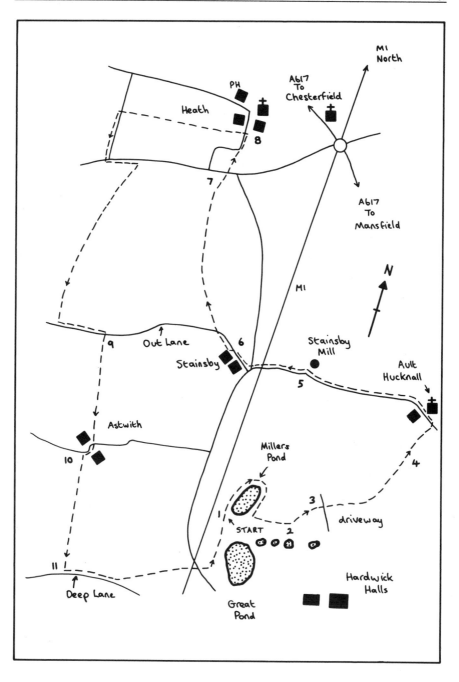

lowed by a footbridge. Now you start to climb back uphill making for a stile in the far right-hand corner of the field. Climb the stile and head half right over to another stile. After this stile you join a track and turn left to walk away from Manor Farm.

10. The track meets a lane on a bend at Astwith. Continue in the same direction. At the second right-hand bend, turn left at a telephone box onto a track. At the first fork keep right and then left at the second fork. The track drops downhill to a stile and then crosses a stream. When the track ends keep over to the right-hand side of the field making for a stile on your right. Follow the right-hand edge of the next field heading towards Ashlea farm to a stile. Climb the stile and walk past the farm on your left and over the next stile onto a track, which leads to Deep Lane.

11. Turn left and follow the lane for several hundred metres. When the lane bends to the right take the path at a public footpath sign off to your left. Follow the left-hand edge of two fields to a plantation. At the plantation turn right in the field corner and at the other side of the plantation there is a stile down a dip on your left. Follow the field edge with a stream on your left, getting ever closer to the M1, and in the field corner turn left onto a track, which leads down onto a road. Turn right and go under the motorway. The car park is off to the left.

Trail 8 – Bolsover Castle

Distance: 12 kilometres/7½ miles

Start: Castle Street Car Park in Bolsover, almost opposite the entrance to Bolsover Castle

Map: OS Explorer 269 Chesterfield and Alfreton

Refreshments: Public houses at Bolsover and Scarcliffe

Toilets: None unless visiting Bolsover Castle

Key Features: Bolsover Castle

Route Instructions

1. Turn left out of the car park exit onto High Street. Pass the Blue Bell Inn on your right and the church on your left. Turn right onto Langwith Road and after 350 metres turn right onto Darwood Lane, which is a rough track lined with private dwelling houses. Keep left as sign-posted at the fork and follow the yellow waymarker to walk to the left of a house before

Bolsover Castle

emerging into open country. Cross two fields to a stile. Climb the stile and in the next field keep to the right-hand side of farm buildings to a gate. Pass through the gate onto a rough lane and turn left at the T-junction into Palterton.

2. When the lane bends sharply to the left keep straight ahead to join a rough track by a public footpath sign. At the end of the track climb a stile and initially keep to the wall on your left. At the end of the wall, continue on a track hedged on both sides heading downhill. Just before the bottom of the track, bear off to the left uphill for 100 metres heading for the top of a ridge. There is no path on the ground, but the route is not difficult to follow for this short space of time. When two stiles 50 metres apart come into view make for the right-hand stile and climb it. Follow the edge of a large field with a fence on the right to a track. Glapwell Lanes Farm can be seen over to the left. Cross the track and leave the field edge to walk straight ahead to a marker post by a hedge. Cross the next field making for a stile next to two trees. Keep to the right of a farm and head for a public footpath sign by a stile.

3. Climb the stile by the houses and turn left onto The Pinfold and left again in 20 metres onto Back Lane. Turn right at the T-junction and enter the grounds of Glapwell FC and Glapwell Colliery Cricket Ground. Turn immediately right to walk with a wall on the right passing first the football pitch and then the cricket ground. Just before the end of the sports ground look out for a public footpath sign off to the right and walk along the edge of a large field with the hedge on the left. Go across the middle of the next field making for a gap in the hedge to join Greer Lane. Turn left and walk to the road.

4. In 20 metres turn right at the crossroads. At the next T-junction turn left as signposted to "Shirebrook". In 200 metres turn left at a public footpath sign. At a fork keep left heading for the edge of Roseland Wood. Ignore the next T- junction of tracks and continue to another T-junction with a hedge in front of you. Turn right and climb a stile in 10 metres. Turn left and left again at the next junction. Cross a footbridge and then bear right to join a path in between the edge of the wood and a wire fence, which soon leads onto Gang Lane. Views of Scarcliffe's St Leonard's Church can be seen to the right.

This late twelfth/early thirteenth century listed building houses the tomb of Constantina Frechville, who died around 1200. The tomb shows Constantina holding a baby. According to legend she lost her way in Scarcliffe Wood and used the ringing church bells to help her find her way back out again. She left five acres of land when she died and the rent from this paid for the curfew

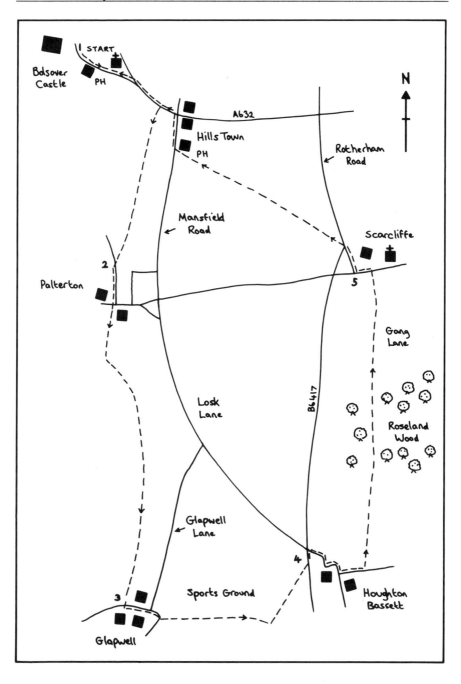

bell to be rung three weeks before Christmas and three weeks after. This tradition is still carried out today.

5. At the end of Gang Lane the route turns left, but if you wish to visit the church turn right and re-trace your steps. In 20 metres turn right and walk up to Rotherham Road. Cross over and climb the stile opposite. The path goes diagonally across two fields to a track. Turn left onto the track and in a few metres bear to the right to head through a gap in a hedge 20 metres ahead. In this field a mound can be seen. Keep to the right-hand side of the mound and follow the clear path across several fields to a sports ground. Cross the sports ground diagonally heading for the road at Hillstown by the "Ace of Clubs". Turn right and at the crossroads turn left to re-trace your steps back to the car park.

Glorious Revolution Country

James II came to the throne in 1685 and soon began to antagonise his Protestant subjects by favouring Catholics and, for example, promoting them to key positions. Three prominent local noblemen, the fourth Earl of Devonshire from Chatsworth House (later created the first Duke of Devonshire for his part in bringing William and Mary to the throne), the Earl of Danby from Kiveton and John Darcy from Aston all rode to meet one another at an alehouse. They began to hatch plans to overthrow James and offer the Crown to his Protestant daughter Mary and her Dutch husband William.

The plans of these three men, along with the birth of a son to James, which pushed Mary's claim to the throne into second place, contributed to Parliament sending a formal invitation and a promise of support to William of Orange to "invade" the country so that Mary could be crowned. Mary, however, refused to accept the Crown unless it was also offered to her husband. William and Mary led a powerful fleet of 250 ships to land at Torbay in Devon on 5 November 1688. By the time they arrived in London they had met with no resistance and James had fled to France. This peaceful invasion has become known in history as The Glorious Revolution. The English landowners in Parliament saw it as "glorious", because there were no English battles and from that time onwards royal power began to decrease, whilst the power of the landowners was on the increase.

The alehouse where the three local noblemen met just outside Chesterfield on the bleak Whittington Moor was called the Cock & Pynot ('pynot' meaning magpie). The former alehouse still stands in the village of Old Whittington and now takes its name, The Revolution House, from The Glorious Revolution of 1688. To commemorate the 250th anniversary of The Glorious Revolution the small cottage was turned into a museum and it is still maintained for this purpose.

Trail 9 – Old Whittington

Distance: 7.3 kilometres/4½ miles

Start: Road side parking on High Street, Old Whittington next to the Revolution House and the Cock & Magpie inn

Map: OS Explorer 269 Chesterfield and Alfreton

Refreshments: Public houses at Old Whittington and Hundall

Toilets: None

Key Features: The Revolution House and views of the Drone valley

Route Instructions

1. From the Revolution House walk past the Cock & Magpie inn and follow the road to The Poplar public house on the right. 75 metres further on, bear right at the fork on to Hundall Lane and climb up to the mast.

2. 50 metres past the mast at the brow of the hill turn left at a public footpath sign and climb a stile. Walk along a field edge with the hedge on the right. At the end of the field continue to follow the hedge round to the right. At a field corner bear half left across the middle of the field to a marker post. Turn right at the marker post to walk with trees on the left. The path then begins to drop down into Ramshaw Wood. Follow the path through the wood for a short while to a marker post and continue straight ahead to Woodsmithies Farm. Here join a track and walk uphill to a road.

3. Cross over the road and turn right to walk into the village of Hundall. At the T-junction by the Miners Arms a public footpath sign can be seen at the other side. Follow the signpost passing a farm on your right to a stile. Climb the stile and continue in the same direction to another stile. Walk across the middle of the next field and climb another stile. Turn left onto a track hedged on both sides and follow it as it bends round to the right. At the corner of Stubbing Wood by a junction of paths keep to the right to walk with the woods on your left for 50 metres to a public footpath sign on the right. Walk across the middle of a field and 50 metres before reaching a lane turn right at a crossroad of paths.

4. Climb a stile by a private dwelling house and continue in the same direction into woodland. Again keep walking in the same direction into an old mining area now colonised by gorse bushes. At the edge of the scrubland

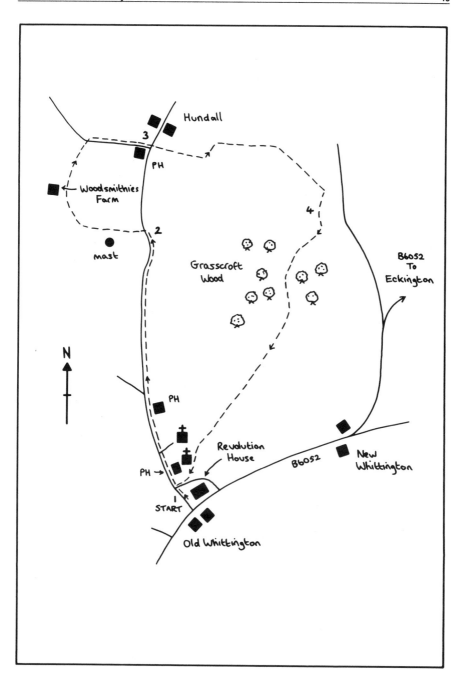

The Revolution House

climb a stile and walk across the middle of a field towards Grasscroft Wood. Climb a ladder stile and walk straight across the woodland. At the other side of the wood the path bears half left and drops downhill across the middle of field. Chesterfield's crooked spire can be seen in the distance. Go through a gate and along a clear path, passing a wooded area on your left, and onto the edge of Whittington. The route goes over a bridge across a stream and then climbs back up to a graveyard on the right. Follow the edge of the graveyard passing the entrance to the church to a lane. Continue straight ahead on a surfaced path, which leads back to the Revolution House.

Trail 10 – Apperknowle ✓

Distance: 7.3 kilometres/4½ miles

Start: Roadside parking on High Street, Apperknowle, near The Yellow Lion.

Map: Explorer 269 Chesterfield and Alfreton

Refreshments: Public houses in Apperknowle, the Black-a-Moor public house on the B6056 and the Gate Inn at Troway

Toilets: None

Key Features: Views over the Drone valley

Route Instructions

1. With your back to The Yellow Lion turn left and walk past Apperknowle Methodist Church. Some 50 metres further on, when the road bends to the right, turn left on to a track. Follow this clear track as it bends to the left and then back to the right before meeting the B6056. Turn left and then immediately right after passing the Black-a-Moor public house and walk into the hamlet of Troway, which was once the home of sickle manufacturers.

2. When the road bends to the right by the Gate Inn climb a stile on the left by a public footpath sign. In 50 metres climb another stile into a field and continue in the same direction to a stile on the edge of woodland. Follow the path through the wood to cross a stream and climb a stile at the other end. Bear to the right for 10 metres and then to the left to walk uphill to a stile and onto a track. Turn right and then bear left at the fork in 50 metres onto a surfaced lane, which you follow to the B6056.

3. Turn right and then left onto Frithwood Road in 100 metres, which is a residential area on the edge of Coal Aston. Follow the road around a right-hand bend and then watch out for a public footpath sign on the left in between Frithwood Close and Frithwood Avenue. After crossing a footbridge, turn immediately to the right to head up some steps into Frith Wood. At the top of the steps there is choice of three paths. Take the right-hand path, which runs fairly close to the river on your right. Keep ahead at a fork and continue to the far side of the wood to meet a track with a sports field beyond it.

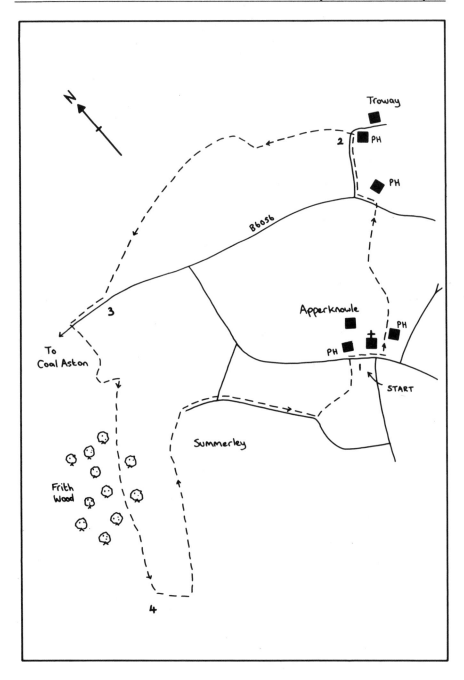

4. Turn left onto the track, which leads to a road. Turn left to head uphill and join a path on the edge of the woodland. Keep on this path ignoring all side turnings and climb steadily uphill until you reach a clear T-junction of tracks at the top. Turn right and walk past Summerley Farm on your right. Walk along Summerley Lower Road with extensive views of the Drone valley to the right. At a T-junction bear left into Apperknowle. Walk straight ahead at a fork onto Chapel Lane and then bear left at the next fork onto Quarry Road. At the top of Quarry Road turn right onto High Street and return to your starting point.

Trail 11 – Monk Wood and Barlow Brook

Distance: 8 kilometres/5 miles

Start: Roadside parking on Highgate Lane, Dronfield, between the Hallowes Golf Clubhouse and Highgate Drive. Hallowes Lane leads directly to Highgate Lane and is off the B6057 by the White Swan public house

Map: Explorer 269 Chesterfield and Alfreton

Refreshments: None

Toilets: None

Key Features: Views over the Drone valley

Route Instructions

1. Follow Highgate Lane to where it bends to the left onto Highgate Drive. Here continue straight ahead onto a bridleway with the Hallowes golf course on your right. There are extensive views across the Drone Valley and of Chesterfield and its crooked spire. Immediately after passing Ouzle Bank Cottage climb over a stile on the right. Follow a field edge with the hedge on your left to a stile. Continue in the same direction to another stile. Climb the stile and join a track. When the track bends to the right up to Bull Close Farm climb a stile on the left and another one in 30 metres. Turn left and follow the field edge round to the right and to a stile in front of some trees.

2. Climb the stile and at the T-junction in front of you turn left and left again in 15 metres to drop downhill through woodland. At the bottom, turn right onto a track.

    In 100 metres turn left at a crossroad of paths and walk down to a bridge over the dual carriageway in between Dronfield and Chesterfield, which was cut through the coal measures. Cross over the bridge and follow the path straight ahead into Monk Wood.

    The wood contains traces of the industrial past. Ironstone was worked here as early as the 12th century and there was a colliery in the wood in the late 19th century.

    At a T-junction turn left and follow the track to Monkwood Farm. Climb a

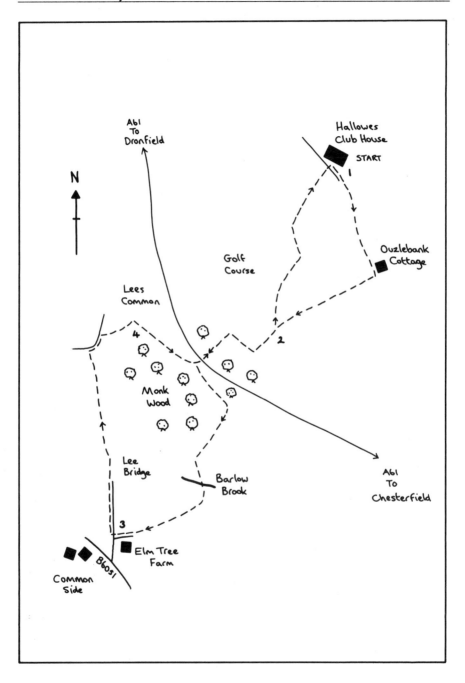

Hallowes golf clubhouse

stile and continue ahead emerging from the woodland and into open country. After crossing Barlow Brook, the track becomes a surfaced lane, which bends to the right and leads to Elm Tree Farm.

The Barlow Brook to Lee Bridge area was used for lead smelting in the 16th and 17th centuries.

By the farm, as the lane bends to the left, turn right onto another lane.

3. This lane drops gently downhill to Lee Bridge over Barlow Brook.

There is a trout fishery on the left, which is on the site of the former Crowhole Colliery.

Cross the brook and continue ahead climbing steeply uphill for a short while. Pass through a gate and emerge at the top of the hill to walk along a field edge with the fence on your right. Pass through another gate and continue along the clear track, which is now hedged on both sides. When the bridleway reaches a lane on a bend keep ahead for 30 metres before turning right over a stile by a public footpath sign. Walk across a field and into woodland. Go over a footbridge and walk steeply uphill across a field to a stile at Lees Common. Climb the stile and turn right to pass through a gate in front of you.

4. Walk with woodland on your left and pass through a gate to re-enter Monk Wood. Continue ahead at a crossroad of tracks and turn left at the next junction. The bridge that you crossed earlier over the dual carriageway can be clearly seen. Retrace your steps over the bridge and back up the hill. Turn right at the crossroad of paths and in 100 metres, still retracing your steps, turn left and walk back up the hill to a stile you crossed earlier. Here instead of climbing the stile, follow the path as it bends to the left and walk with the golf course on your left to a T-junction of tracks. Turn left and then right in 150 metres onto a track. The golf course and extensive views of Sheffield are on the left. This track leads to Highgate Lane by the golf club house. Turn right and return to the starting point.

The golf club house was originally Hallowes Hall, which was built in 1657.

Into the Industrial Revolution

The Moss Valley

The river Moss and the surrounding valley offer an opportunity to explore the remains of industries past in a beautiful woodland setting, which has become a haven for wildlife. This quiet wooded valley has not always been as peaceful as it is now, because from the 15th century through to the 19th century it was an important centre and hive of activity for the people of Ford, Ridgeway, Eckington and Mosborough for the sickle and scythe industry. The river provided the source of power to drive the wheels for grinding and forging and at one time there were eight wheels in use. Although there are no remains of the old works, the dams can still be seen. The goods produced were exported to the West Indies and the United States.

Coal was also once mined here in shallow drift mines and a tramway, the embankment of which can still be seen, took coal to the coking ovens at Plumbley up until the mid-19th century. The derelict engine house of the Seldom Seen mine can still be seen.

This "ancient" woodland contains a mixture of broad-leaved trees, such as, oak, English elm and sycamore. There is a great variety of plant life, for example, bluebells, dog's mercury, wood anemones, wild garlic and lesser celandine. The area is also of great interest to birdwatchers with kingfishers, herons, tree-creepers, green woodpeckers and sparrowhawks all to be found. The river is one of the least polluted in the region and trout can be found in secluded stretches.

Ridgeway Cottage Industry Centre

In Trail 13, we visit Ridgeway Cottage Industry Centre: a 300-year-old restored farm situated in the attractive village of Ridgeway in the heart of the Moss Valley, which has now earned a reputation amongst tourists and local visitors as a place to browse and shop for a wide range of quality goods. Traditional and modern crafts are brought to life in a complex of workshops and studios, which was opened in 1987.

Kent House Farm was constructed in the second half of the 1700s and remained as a working farm until the Council bought it in a somewhat poor state from Jessica Hutton in 1985. Little is known about the early history of the farm or the people who worked the land, but it certainly provided a focal point in the village of Ridgeway. The farm itself was a product of the Enclosure Acts. During the 1800s, the estate passed through various families (Jenkin, Wilson and Hutton). The last people to work the farm were two generations of the Marsh family.

Ashover

Ashover, meaning ash tree slope, is set in the beautiful Amber Valley, the valley of "silence and wildflowers", surrounded by tree clad hillsides. The village is one of the prettiest in Derbyshire and although it lies just outside the Peak National Park it could be described as a typical Peak District village. Ashover appears in the Domesday Book and was probably in existence 200 years before that. The focal point of the village and a prominent landmark is its church surrounded by many old cottages built of local limestone and gritstone.

The whole area was once an important lead-mining centre and there is much evidence of the old time mining. The geology is a mixture of millstone grit, carboniferous limestone and volcanic tuff. It is a region rich in fossils and mineral deposits, such as, fluorspar, lead and building stone. 'Rakes' are the main types of mineral vein seen in the area. These are straight veins of ore between vertical walls of surrounding rock.

Reservoirs

The Linacre Reservoirs provide a majestic and delightful setting for Trail 17. The Lower Reservoir was built as a result of an Act of Parliament passed in 1855. It is 9.45 metres deep, 3.44 hectares in size and holds 140.9 million litres of water. Then an Act passed in 1885 resulted in the construction of the Upper Reservoir. This reservoir is 18.75 metres deep, 7.29 hectares in size and holds 575 million litres. Finally, an Act of Parliament in 1904 lead to the building of the Middle reservoir. This is 12.9 metres deep, 6.9 hectares in size and holds 410.9 million litres of water.

Up until 1909 the water was simply stored and piped to customers, however, complaints about the taste and odour led to the installation of filter beds. A quote of the time regarding the quality of the water said that the poor used it as soup, the middle class for washing their clothes and the elite for watering their gardens. In 1909 the water was supplied to 70,000 local people in the area. As the current population could not be satisfied by the supply of water from the Linacre Reservoirs their demand is met from various Derbyshire reservoirs.

For nearly 500 years the Linacre woodlands were part of a busy industrial landscape. The woods conceal archaeological evidence of quarrying, lead smelting and iron production and milling.

Rother Valley Country Park

This was opened in 1983 on what, until the 1970s, had been a major open-cast coal site. The park is centred on a series of lakes, the river Rother and the early 17th century historic Bedgreave Mill, which now acts as a visitor centre. The range of facilities in the park is endless, such as, the popular watersports centre catering for windsurfing, jet-skiing, cable water-skiing and the sailing of model boats. Other potential leisure pursuits are cycling, angling or the golf course including a driving range. There is also a nature reserve, which has been allowed to establish itself naturally.

The park acts as a major migratory route for birds and it is a valuable over wintering site for flocks of teal, tufted duck and canada geese.

There are numerous extension plans in the pipeline including linking the park into the Chesterfield Canal, which is currently undergoing restoration.

The Five Pits Trail

This is an 8-mile scenic route, which winds across rolling countryside linking five former large, deep Derbyshire colliery sites at Tibshelf, Pilsley, Holmewood, Williamthorpe and Grassmoor. It also passes through the sites of smaller collieries at Pewit, Alma and Lings and several traditional mining villages. At first, this proposition may not appear very attractive, but Derbyshire County Council, the Countryside Ranger Service and various local groups have quickly brought the disused land back to life and there is plenty of historical interest coupled with fine views.

The growth of coal mining in the middle of the 19th century was soon followed by the development of mineral railways, which meant that coal could easily be transported to the main railway lines. All the coal seams had been worked out and the collieries and railway lines were all closed by 1973. Derbyshire County Council then constructed the trail between 1979 and 1989 as part of its Derelict Land Reclamation Project. The northern loop of the trail is constructed on the original track bed of the mineral lines, while the southern length was part of the Great Central Line, which once linked the area with London. The former collieries have now been transformed into woodland and meadows providing a haven for an ever-increasing variety of wildlife. Grassmoor Country Park at the northern end of the trail was reclaimed from the spoil heaps and railway sidings of the Grassmoor colliery and is now beginning to mature.

Trail 12 – The Moss Valley: East ✓

Distance: 9.5 kilometres/6 miles

Start: A car park down a track in front of the Bridge Inn at Ford near Ridgeway – the Ford picnic site and Angling Club

Map: OS Explorer 278 Sheffield & Barnsley

Refreshments: Bridge Inn at Ford and public houses at Mosborough

Toilets: None

Key Features: A section of The Mosborough Country Walk, Eckington Hall & Mosborough Hall

Route Instructions

1. From the car park cross a footbridge and join a track. Bear left to the road by the Bridge Inn to the pleasant hamlet of Ford, where for generations several families were involved in farming and the sickle and scythe industry. Turn right and walk uphill for 200 metres before turning right again onto a bridle path. This walk twists and turns around the Moss Valley providing extensive views from different elevations.

Mosborough Hall

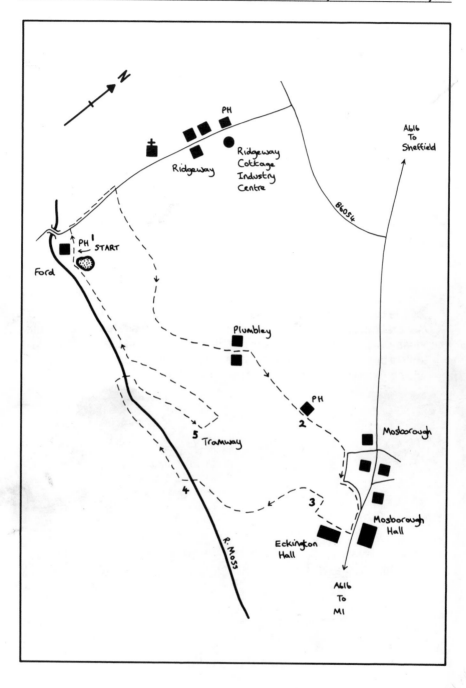

At a crossroad of tracks turn right. At the next junction, keep straight ahead and follow the track as it bends to the left and later to the right into the hamlet of Plumbley. Plumbley may mean "an open place for smelting". At the end of the houses in Plumbley turn right at the crossroad of tracks and walk towards the houses of Mosborough passing Plumbley Lane Farm on your right.

2. On reaching the road The Wheel public house is on your left. At the T-junction turn right and follow the road as it bends to the left. Take the next right onto Chapel Street passing Mosborough Methodist church on your left, which was built in 1888. After 100 metres turn left at a T-junction and bear left at the next junction. A right turn at yet another T-junction brings you onto the A616 (High Street). Pass the George and Dragon on your left and then on a right-hand bend Mosborough Hall Hotel, built around 1625, is on the left. Shortly after a house called Elmwood turn right at a public footpath sign to walk up a narrow path called the Pingle, which separates Elmwood and Eckington Hall between two high walls. Eckington Hall is a few metres beyond the public footpath sign.

Both properties were constructed by the Wells family, who were local coal barons, Elmwood was built in 1881 and Eckington Hall in 1871.

3. On reaching a lane turn right and then left in 15 metres at a public footpath sign up a track walled on both sides. Cross a stile and head down into a field. At the end of the hedge on your left look out for a stile over to your left at the corner of a plantation of trees (Ladybank Wood). Climb the stile and head diagonally across the field to a stile in the far right-hand corner and just down a dip. Walk along a field edge with the hedge on your right to a T-junction of paths. Turn right to walk along a path hedged on both sides. At a fork bear left to a footbridge, which is 50 metres ahead of you and cross over the River Moss.

4. At a crossroad of tracks turn right to walk through Twelve Acre Wood. Keep right at the next two forks. On your left is open ground. Cross over a footbridge and turn right and immediately right again over a stile to double back on yourself and walk with the river on your right. The path heads uphill and emerges at the edge of the wood at a stile. Climb the stile and follow the hedge along the topside of the wood until you reach a stile to enter trees in front of you.

5. After the stile turn left at a junction of tracks and head gently uphill.

This sunken track was the line of the old tramway, known locally as the "drag road", where coal was hauled from the Footrail colliery in the valley bottom to the weighbridge at Plumbley.

In 100 metres when a path crosses the track turn left and head across to a field corner and a stile shortly afterwards. Drop downhill and continue in the same direction crossing two stiles before the path cuts back into woodland to another stile. Climb the stile and take the middle of three tracks to another stile. Turn right, passing a dam on your right. By a small waterfall cross a footbridge over a stream and follow the path across several stiles to the Mill Pond and car park at Ford. The Mill Pond is frequented by a local Angling Club.

Trail 13 – The Moss Valley: West

Distance: 6.5 kilometres/4 miles

Start: Roadside parking on Main Road through Ridgeway opposite Ridgeway Craft Centre and near The Swan public house

Maps: OS Explorer 278 Sheffield & Barnsley

Refreshments: Public houses in Ridgeway and Ford

Toilets: None

Key Features: Part of the Moss Valley and Ridgeway Cottage Industry Centre

Route Instructions

1. Follow the public footpath sign by the side of The Swan public house passing Ridgeway House built in 1750 on your left. At the end of the housing enter a field. Walk across the middle of two fields to a wall corner and climb a stile. The path drops diagonally downhill to a T-junction of paths by a tree. Here turn right onto Robinbrook Lane. In quick succession cross a footbridge, a stile and another footbridge and continue along the track hedged on both sides next to Robin Brook to a T-junction by a marker post. This path can become very muddy. Turn left and shortly afterwards climb a stile.

2. In 20 metres there is a choice of three paths. Take the middle path heading half right to a stile passing Carterhall Farm. Climb the stile and follow a field edge with a hedge on your left to the edge of Ryall's Wood. Turn right in front of the wood to walk downhill with the wood on your left. The path then crosses a brook and heads uphill across a field towards Povey Farm. At a signpost by a wall at the farm turn left to walk with a wall on the left and farm buildings on the right. At a junction of paths, continue ahead.

3. 100 metres past the farm leave the track at a right-hand bend. There is no signpost, therefore, take care not to miss the route. Walk along a field edge with the hedge on your left. After several hundred metres the path turns right and heads diagonally across the middle of the field towards the other end of Ryall's Wood. The path enters the woodland and follows the right-hand edge of the wood down to a junction of tracks. Here turn left and immediately walk over stepping-stones across the brook. A path hedged on both sides heads up to Geerlane Farm.

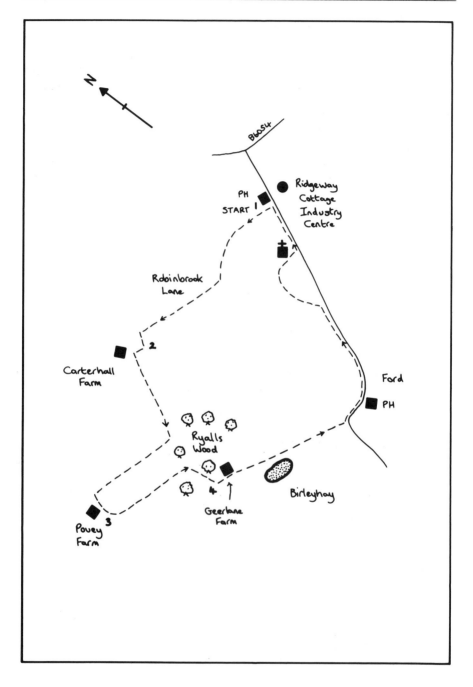

4. Turn right at a T-junction, which is sign posted a "Country Walk To Ford" to join a clear surfaced lane which leads to Birleyhay and passes the Mill Pond on the right. Continue on until reaching the road at Ford. Turn left and pass the Bridge Inn on your right. The road bends to the left and heads uphill into Ridgeway. After 250 metres turn left onto Sloade Lane. At the bottom of the hill, cross a ford. 50 metres further on turn right at a marker post, cross a brook and climb steeply up a series of steps. At a junction turn right onto a surfaced track to arrive back at Main Road through Ridgeway by the side of the church of St John the Evangelist. Turn left and return to the Cottage Industry Centre after several hundred metres.

Trail 14 – The Moss Valley: South

Distance: 7.3 kilometres/4½ miles

Start: Roadside parking on the B6056 at Coal Aston near the Royal Oak public house and the village hall

Maps: OS Pathfinder 743 (SK28/38) Sheffield; Explorer 269 Chesterfield and Alfreton

Refreshments: The Royal Oak and the nearby Chequers Inn at Coal Aston

Toilets: None

Key Features: Part of the Moss Valley

Route Instructions

1. Standing with your back to the Royal Oak turn right and take the second public footpath sign to the right virtually opposite Stone Road. Drop down some steps and walk in between houses to a crossroads. Continue straight ahead onto Shaw Street and at the T- junction with Wilson Road cross over to the public footpath sign opposite. You soon leave the housing behind and walk to a stile. Climb it and walk along a field edge with the hedge on your right. Climb two more stiles and turn right at the T-junction with Cross Lane.

2. After passing a private lane on your left the track bends to the left and starts to head towards Nor Wood across the middle of a field. At a T- junction turn left to walk directly towards the woodland. The path runs gently downhill through the wood to a footbridge. Cross the footbridge and turn immediately right at the T-junction into Long Wood. Bear left in 50 metres and left again 50 metres further on to emerge shortly afterwards at the edge of the wood by a stile with Hazlebarrow Farm in the distance. Walk along a field edge with the hedge on the left to a hedge corner. Keep straight ahead to a gate and stile in 50 metres. Climb the stile and follow a track hedged on both sides to the edge of the farm buildings.

There was once a hall here, having being the home of the Hazlebarrows since the thirteenth century. It was demolished in 1810.

3. Just in front of the farm, although there is no signpost, turn right through a gate onto a bridleway, with instructions to carefully fasten the gate, and walk along a field edge with the hedge on your right. At the other end of

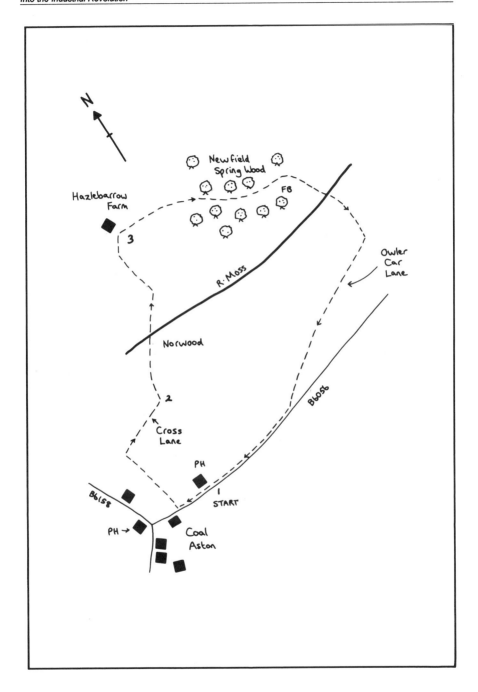

the field pass through another gate and follow the winding edge of New-field Spring Wood to a footbridge. Cross the footbridge and bear to the right uphill and right again to follow the edge of woodland down to the River Moss. Cross the river and walk to the edge of the woodland. Turn left and then right. The bridleway is to the left of the field and continues uphill to the junction with Owler Car Lane. Turn right and follow the clear track back to the B6056. Turn right again and return to the Royal Oak.

Trail 15 – Ashover & Cocking Tor

Distance: 9 kilometres/5½ miles

Start: Car Park in Ashover on Church Street, which is sign posted off the B6036

Map: OS Explorer 269 Chesterfield and Alfreton

Refreshments: Public houses at Ashover

Toilets: Sign posted near the Black Swan Inn

Key Features: The village of Ashover, Goss Hall, Overton Hall and Cocking Tor

Route Instructions

1. Bear left out of the car park and left again at the next junction by the Black Swan public house.

The Crispin Inn and the church are on the right. This Inn's alleged history is announced on a large board on the property, which claims to date the premises to the time of Agincourt in 1415, but it is more likely to be from the 17th century like many other buildings in the parish. A church at Ashover is mentioned in the Domesday Book, but nothing remains of the original building. The present All Saints Church was constructed between 1350 and 1419. It has many interesting tombs and brasses. For example, it houses the alabaster tomb of Thomas Babington and his wife. In the churchyard, there are four tombs in memory of the Nightingale family. Florence Nightingale, the infamous "Lady of the Lamp" from the Crimean War once lived at nearby Dethick.

Immediately after the church turn right at a public footpath sign. Follow the path to a sports field. Walk along the edge of the field with the wall on the left to a gap in a wall corner. Go through the gap and continue to the B6036.

2. Turn left onto the road and right in 20 metres onto a track There is no signpost but a large metal gate can be seen 20 metres ahead. Pass the side of the gate and immediately climb a stile into a field. Head downhill passing close to the trackbed of the now dismantled Ashover Light Railway, as shown on the Ordnance Survey map.

The 7.5-mile narrow gauge line was built between 1922 and 1925 by the Clay

Cross Company to transport fluorspar and limestone from its quarries at Ashover and nearby Milltown. A Ministry of Defence Directive instructed the railway to provide a full passenger service from the isolated Ashover. Unfortunately, a bus service was soon introduced and this effectively killed the passenger service. The quarrying ended in 1950 and the railway line was closed.

On reaching a hedge follow it round to the right and to a stile. Climb the stile and then cross the footbridge over Marsh Brook, and then go over another stile.

3. Continue ahead up a track. Just in front of the entrance to a quarry and a footbridge turn right to walk with the quarry on the left. Cross two tracks within 100 metres and keep in the same direction to a footbridge over the River Amber. Bear left and walk with the river on your left along two field edges to a stile at the side of a gate. Follow the right-hand edge of a field to a gap in the far right corner. Immediately pass through another gap and keep straight ahead across a field to a lane passing Goss Hall on the right.

Goss Hall was transferred from the Deincourt family to the Babington's. Until a recent renovation, it had stood for many years in ruins. Anthony Babington, the great, great grandson of Thomas Babington, whose tomb is in Ashover church, was the ringleader of the famous Babington Plot to assassinate Queen Elizabeth I, replace her with Mary Stuart (Mary Queen of Scots) and foster the Catholic movement. When Elizabeth I discovered the plot, Anthony reputedly hid in the cellar at Goss Hall. He was, however, eventually arrested, tried for treason and faced a most gruesome death. Mary was herself charged with an involvement in the plot for which she too was tried and executed.

4. Turn left onto the lane. Pass a farm on the right and then turn right at a public footpath sign opposite the next building on the lane. Keep to the right of a barn and head uphill in a long narrow field. At the top of the field the path bears to the right to a stile at the side of a gate. Climb the stile into woodland and follow the clear path to emerge from the trees and continue to a road. Turn left and pass Old Engine Farm on the right.

The site of the farm became the main pumping station for the Gregory Mine, which was once one of the main mines in the area. Views of Riber Castle can also be seen in the distance over to the right.

Just after Old Engine Farm turn left at a public footpath sign onto a track on the edge of a field. The track leads to a small plantation. Keep to the outside right-hand edge of the plantation round to a corner on the other

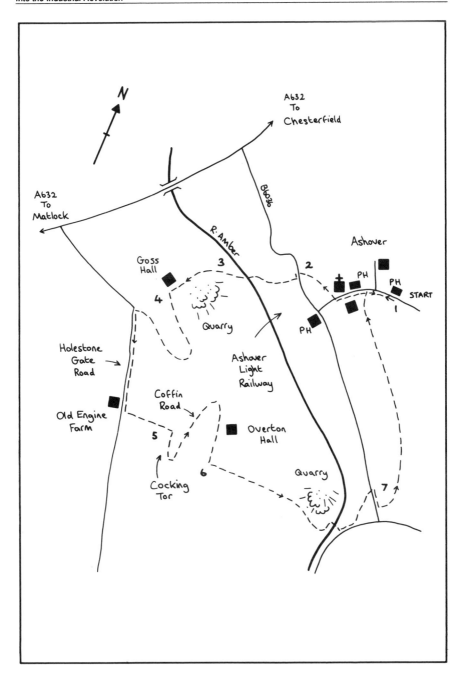

side and bear half right over to the far right-hand corner of the field to a gap in the wall. Pass through the gap and turn right almost immediately onto a ridge top path.

The path reaches Cocking Tor in about 100 metres, where there is a fine view of Ogston Reservoir. This man-made lake was made by the flooding of the valley to provide water for the NCB carbonisation plant at Wingerworth in 1956, which at the time was the largest in Europe. The reservoir is now a haven for sailing and angling.

5. Follow the path along the edge of the ridge by Cocking Tor, which soon begins to climb steeply downhill along a rocky path. Turn left on meeting a T-junction of paths and keep left again at a fork in a few metres. Turn left onto a track and follow this over old workings dropping down to another track just before it leads into woodland.

This track is known as the Coffin Road and is a former packhorse road so called because corpses were brought from outlying villages, which did not have their own burial grounds.

Shortly after emerging from the woodland turn right at a large crossroads of tracks. Pass Overton Hall on the left.

Overton Hall was handed down from the Overton family to the Hunt's in 1327. The house later came into the ownership of the Hodgkinson's in 1599. There are two date stones set in the boundary wall to William (WEH1699) and Elizabeth (HW+E1702) Hodgkinson who owned the hall at the time. The hall then passed to the Banks family. Sir Joseph Banks was a naturalist who sailed with Captain Cook on his Endeavour. In 1918, The Clay Cross Company purchased the estate. They had no interest in the hall itself as they wished to commercially exploit the fluorspar and limestone deposits. To transport the minerals the Ashover Light Railway was constructed. Overton Hall is now a private residence.

6. At a crossroad of tracks turn left. When this track becomes a surfaced lane and bends to the right, keep straight ahead onto a path by a public footpath signpost. Ignore any paths to the right and follow the outside edge of a quarry round to a footbridge over the River Amber and onto a lane. Turn left onto the lane and at a T-junction turn left. Do not cross the bridge over the river, but walk ahead onto a track and up to a gate to a private residence. Turn left onto a path walking with the river on the left. Cross a track and continue to a lane.

7. Turn right and in 50 metres look out for steps on the left by a public footpath signpost. Climb the steps into a field with a bungalow in front of you. Keep to the left following the edge of a quarry. After passing through a gap beside a gate turn left into woodland. Keep in the same direction across a small field picking up a clear path. On reaching, a large field turn right to follow the field edge with the wall on the right. Pass through a gap in the wall and walk straight ahead across a number of fields back to Ashover. Turn right on meeting the road opposite the Crispin Inn and right again at the T-junction by the Black Swan.

Church at Ashover

Trail 16 – Ashover & Bole Hill

Distance: 10.5 kilometres/6½ miles

Start: Car Park in Ashover on Church Street, which is sign posted off the B6036

Map: OS Explorer 269 Chesterfield and Alfreton

Refreshments: Public houses at Ashover

Toilets: Signposted from near the Black Swan Inn

Key Features: The village of Ashover, the Press Reservoirs, a section of the South Chesterfield Way and Eastwood Hall

Route Instructions

1. Turn left out of the car park. In 50 metres, turn right through a gate at a public footpath signpost into a field. Initially walk across the middle of the field by the markers and then by the field edge to a gate. Follow an uphill path to a lane. Turn left and in 50 metres climb a stile on the right. Continue uphill in the same direction to a path that runs across the top of the ridge and rocky Fabric outcrop. Cross over this path to reach a lane at a T-junction. Take the road ahead sign posted to Alton. In Alton turn left at the T-junction. At the next junction bear left and cross over the lane to a signed public footpath. The path soon becomes a track, which passes a quarry on the left. Continue across fields in the same direction to a lane at Northedge.

2. Turn left onto the lane and in 100 metres turn right at a public footpath sign. In a few metres bear right to a stile, which can be seen to the left and rear of a building. Climb the stile and head over to the right to a track. In 20 metres, turn left onto this track to follow it across a field and along the top edge of the middle of the three Press Reservoirs. After the reservoirs bear to the right in the field you have entered and follow it to its tapered end, which leads onto a path through trees to a stile. Climb the stile and walk across the middle of the field to a stile. After the stile turn right onto a track. On reaching a lane turn left and pass Bole Hill Farm on the left. When the lane bends to the left at the top of the hill turn right at a public footpath sign into woodland and join the South Chesterfield Way.

Bole Hill Quarry shown on the map indicates that this was a site of a bole or bloomery for smelting iron-ore and lead in Medieval or Tudor times.

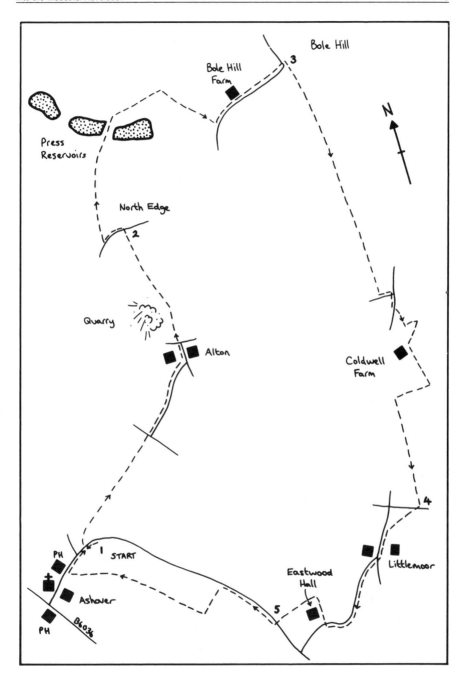

Bole Hill

Bole Hill
Farm

3

Press
Reservoirs

N

North Edge

2

Quarry

Alton

Coldwell
Farm

7

4

PH
1 START

Littlemoor

Eastwood
Hall

5

Ashover

PH

B6036

The view from Eastwood Hall to Cocking Tor

3. Follow the clear path along the right-hand side of the woodland. At the end of the wood the path continues along field edges into Britton Wood. Immediately on entering the wood take the left fork and continue to a lane. Turn left and then right at a T-junction. In 30 metres turn left onto a lane, which bends first to the left and then to the right up to Coldwell Farm. Leave the South Chesterfield Way for a short while and pass in front of the farm to walk along a grass track by a field edge. At the end of the field follow the track into the next field for 20 metres and then turn right onto an uphill path, which climbs up to the top of the ridge. Turn left onto a track back on the South Chesterfield Way and keep in the same direction along field edges to a lane.

4. Here leave the South Chesterfield Way and turn right onto the lane sign posted for Littlemoor. 50 metres before a crossroads climb a stile on the left into a field by a public footpath sign. Walk diagonally across the field to a stile, which leads onto a road. Turn left to walk through the village of Littlemoor.

There are fine views of Ogston Reservoir over to the left. This man-made lake was made by the flooding of the valley to provide water for the NCB carbonisation plant at Wingerworth in 1956, which at the time was the largest in Europe. The reservoir is now a haven for sailing and angling.

Just past the Methodist church bear right at a fork by Lanes End bungalow. This rough lane drops downhill and bends to the right.

Views of the ruins of Eastwood Hall come into sight. This Hall was in existence in the early thirteenth century, but it has stood in ruins since 1646 when the Roundheads all but destroyed it in the Civil War.

Close to the Hall turn right at a public footpath sign into the farmyard. Go through a gap and follow a path to the left around the farm buildings and across fields to emerge at a lane by the side of Eastwood House Farm.

5. Turn right onto the lane and in 100 metres go through a gap in a wall on the left at a public footpath sign. Cross the middle of a field and pass through another gap in a wall. Walk along the right-hand edge of a field. At the end of the field turn right and follow a path in the direction of the church spire emerging onto the road by the Crispin Inn in Ashover. Turn right and right again onto Church Street by the Black Swan.

Trail 17 – Linacre Reservoirs

Distance: 8 kilometres/5 miles

Start: Linacre Reservoirs sign posted off the B5050 in between Cutthorpe and Ingmanthorpe. There are three small car parks in very close proximity. First one on the right, then one on the left and the bottom car park is on the right

Maps: OS Explorer 269 Chesterfield and Alfreton; OS Outdoor Leisure 24 The Peak District White Peak Area

Refreshments: George and Dragon public house at Old Brampton

Toilets: Linacre Reservoirs

Key Features: Linacre Reservoirs and the village of Old Brampton

Route Instructions

1. From the bottom car park turn right and follow the lane down past the toilet block. Glimpses of the Lower Reservoir can be seen over to the right. When the lane ends continue along a rough track. Cross over Linacre Brook and keep straight ahead. Emerge from the woodland onto a track hedged on both sides. Again keep in the same direction at Woodnook to a road. Turn left onto the road.

2. In 75 metres turn right at a public bridleway sign. This clear track crosses a stream and passes Broomhall Farm on the right. Immediately after the farm turn right at a T-junction of tracks. The track gradually climbs uphill to meet the road through Old Brampton. Turn left and follow the road through the village of pretty cottages and exclusive houses.

You pass the Church of St Peter and Paul on your right, which is of Norman origins. Strangely, the church clock face shows 63 minutes! Opposite the attractive church is Brampton Hall, a 12th century building of great historical interest, with cruck old beams and timbers allegedly from an earlier village church.

At the other end of the village, the pavement rises along a grassy bank. At the side of Holly Cottage, turn right at a public footpath sign.

3. Climb a stile at the end of a building into a field. Walk along the field edge with a wall on the right to a stile. Continue in the same direction in the next field to a stile. In the next field, turn right over a stile in 30 metres and walk

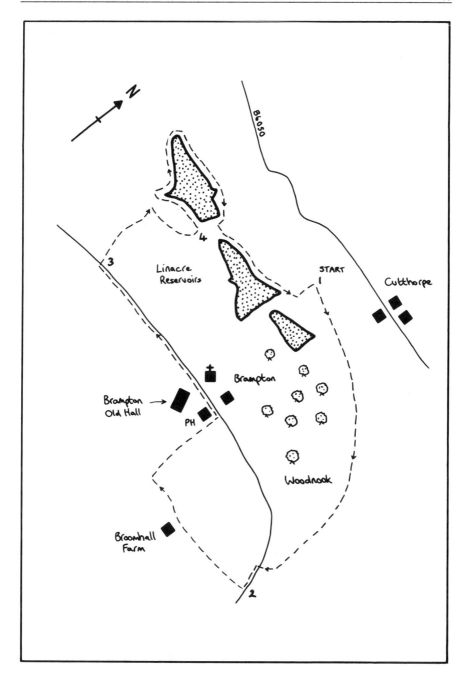

The church at Old Brampton

diagonally across the field to a stile by the corner of woodland. Climb the stile and walk along a field edge with the wall on the right to another stile. In 50 metres after the stile, a signpost instructs you to turn right. Walk along a field edge with views of the Upper Reservoir and climb a stile into woodland. Drop down to the dam wall of the Upper Reservoir. There is a picnic area here.

4. Turn left to walk along the man-made path next to the reservoir and back round to the other side of the upper dam wall. Shortly afterwards bear right to follow a winding track down to the side of the Middle Reservoir. Walk alongside the reservoir, passing another picnic place, to its dam wall. Continue for 75 metres beyond the dam wall and turn left up a path to climb steps back to the lower car park.

Trail 18 – Holmesfield and Millthorpe

Distance: 8 kilometres/5 miles

Start: The bottom of Millthorpe Lane (small parking area) at the junction with the B6051 at Millthorpe near the Royal Oak public house

Map: OS Outdoor Leisure 24 The Peak District White Peak Area

Refreshments: The Royal Oak at Millthorpe, various public houses at Holmesfield and The Robin Hood on the B6054 near Lidgate.

Toilets: None

Key Features: Holmesfield, Woodthorpe Hall, Totley Brook and Fanshaw Old Hall

---

Holmesfield is an ancient parish situated on the foothills of the Pennines, which in medieval times was part of the Bakewell parish. Later it was transferred to the parish of Dronfield before finally achieving autonomy in 1857. The main village sits on a ridge top overlooking several smaller hamlets, such as Millthorpe.

Route Instructions

1. Walk up Millthorpe Lane towards Holmesfield passing Nethershude Nurseries on the left. In 100 metres turn left at the public bridleway sign for Horlseygate Lane. Immediately there is a choice of two routes. Bear right over a stile into a field. Walk along two field edges with a stream on the left. In the third field look out for a footbridge over the stream. Cross the footbridge and continue in the same direction as previously now walking with the stream on the right, heading towards the village of Holmesfield on the ridge top. Climb two stiles in quick succession and continue uphill to another stile. Follow the left-hand edge of the field to a stile by a gate, which leads to a track. The track reaches the B6054 at Holmesfield by the side of The George and Dragon, which at one time was both a farmhouse and an alehouse.

One of the striking things about Holmesfield is the number of public houses there are within a short distance of one another. This is because the road was a turnpike road in 1845 and it was a convenient stopping off place for many routes. St Swithens Church is on the opposite side of the road. There has been a church on this site since Anglo-Saxon times, but the present church was built in 1826. The church shares the natural ridge site with the medieval motte (mound) and surrounding ditch from which Castle Hill takes its name.

2. Turn left and in 40 metres turn right onto Park Avenue, which is sign posted to Woodthorpe Hall and Totley at the side of the The Angel.

The present inn was built on the site of a much older building, which had been church property until a brewery purchased it in the 1950s. On the left of Park Avenue is Holmesfield Hall Farm. The original hall may now be on the site of private dwellings, but the present hall contains a 1613 datestone, with its facade added in the 18th century by the Burton family. The coat of arms of the Burton's can be seen. This was the crest given to James Burton, a squire of Richard I for his bravery at the siege of Cyprus.

At the end of the surfaced lane climb a stile at the side of a bungalow and follow the clear path into Holmesfield Park Wood.

This ancient woodland was once a deer park, but it now forms part of the Woodthorpe estate.

Continue in the same direction through the wood ignoring any other paths until reaching a lane at the other end of the wood.

3. Turn right along the lane, which leads to Woodthorpe Hall.

This 17th century house was erected by the Fanshaws who moved here from Fanshaw Gate Hall, which is passed later on this walk. Indeed many of the materials for Woodthorpe Hall were taken from the Fanshaws' previous home. It became derelict in the 1920s, but has subsequently been restored by the Shepley family.

At the end of the lane continue straight ahead onto a path by a public foot-path sign. This path soon turns into two paths running along side one another and either route can be taken as both eventually drop down to a wide track. Turn right onto the track and 100 metres before meeting Mickley Lane at Totley look out for a path crossing the track and turn left.

4. Cross a footbridge and just in front of housing turn left along a path beside Totley Brook. Climb a stile and keep left along the side of the brook to another stile. Continue on and keep straight ahead at a crossroad of tracks with a footbridge on the left. In 400 metres turn left onto a path which drops down to another footbridge over the brook. Walk uphill to a wall and continue climbing along a field edge making for Fanshaw Gate, which can be seen over to the right. Pass in between two gateposts and bear round to the left to a lane. Turn right onto the lane.

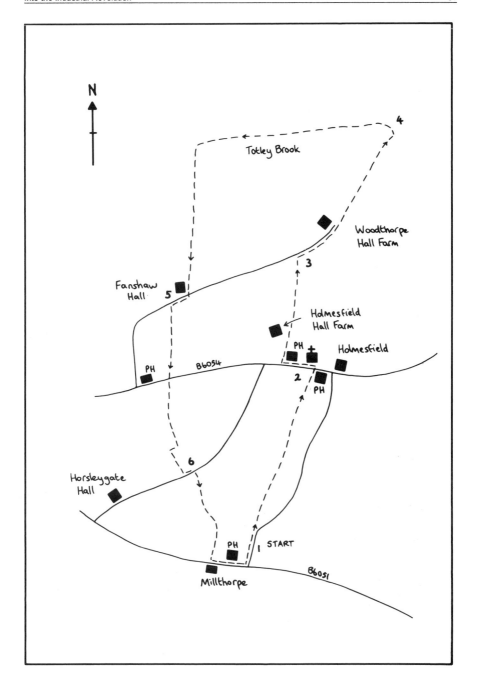

Fanshaw Gate Hall stands behind an imposing set of gate pillars. The notable local Fanshaw family built this once large and important house as their main seat after leasing the land from Beauchief Abbey in 1260. The Hall is a fraction of its previous size, as Robert Fanshaw first reduced it in 1636 and then it was partly demolished in the 17th century when the Fanshaws moved to Woodthorpe Hall. Although the Fanshaws did not continue to reside at Fanshaw Gate the property remained, often let, with the family until 1944 when it was sold for the first time.

5. In 75 metres turn left at a public footpath sign. Follow the path walking with fencing on the right steadily up hill to a signpost. Here keep straight ahead to the B6054.

To the right the Robin Hood Inn can be seen. This early 19th century small alehouse was extended with the turnpiking of the road and the construction of a nearby tollhouse.

Cross over the road to the public footpath signpost. Follow the yellow waymarkers round to the right and then to the left. Climb a stile on the right and cut diagonally across a field corner to another stile. Walk across the middle of the next field to a yellow waymarker by a stile.

The Royal Oak, Millthorpe

Chesterfield and its crooked spire can be seen in the distance over to the left.

Walk along a field edge with the fence on the left to a stile. Climb the stile and, at the next field corner, turn right at a public footpath sign. Follow the field edge round to the left to a gate. Walk with a holly hedge on the left down to a Horsleygate Lane.

A detour to the right down this lane can be taken to view Horsleygate Hall. The hall is a grade two listed building and although it is unclear exactly when it was erected some parts of the building date back to the 15th century. In 1806 the hall was very badly damaged by fire and it remained in a very poor state of repair until a recent renovation.

6. Turn left onto the lane for 15 metres and then right over a stile onto a caravan site. Walk along the main track through the site and when the track bends to the right keep ahead to a stile into a field. Drop downhill to the far left-hand corner of the field by a stream. Pass through a gap by a gate, cross a footbridge and turn right after a stile. In a few metres, at a public footpath sign to Millthorpe, walk half left across the middle of a field. On reaching two gates, pass through the gate on the left to walk along a field edge with the hedge on the right. Just before the corner of the field climb a stile on the right. Walk across the middle of the field slightly to the left to a stile. In the next field, head towards the side of a house to reach the B6051. Turn left and just after The Royal Oak, turn left at the T-junction.

Trail 19 – Holmesfield and The Cordwell Valley

Distance: 6.5 kilometres/4 miles

Start: Public footpath in between 51 and 53 Gosforth Drive, Gosforth Valley, Dronfield. Near the Coach and Horses public house on Sheffield Road (B6057) turn onto Stubley Hollows, which leads to Stubley Lane and onto Carr Lane. Turn left onto Pentland Road and left again onto Gosforth Drive. The footpath is close to Draycott Place

Map: OS Outdoor Leisure 24 The Peak District White Peak Area

Refreshments: None

Toilets: None

Key Features: Extensive views of the Cordwell and Cowley valleys where small-scale coal mining once took place and the two Cartledge Halls

Route Instructions

1. Take the public footpath in between 51 and 53 Gosforth Drive. After the housing a signpost can be seen over to the left. Take the path indicated for Barlow Lees. When the path bends to the left, bear right down some steps and climb a stile. Walk downhill to a footbridge. Cross the footbridge and continue ahead along several field edges with the hedge on your left to a lane at Cowley. Turn right and pass Cowley Mission chapel built in 1893 on your right.

2. Just after the chapel turn left at a public footpath sign onto a track fenced on both sides. Bear right over a brook and follow a field edge with the hedge on the left. Follow the field corner round to the right and in 15 metres turn left down steps and across a footbridge. Follow a field edge passing Lees Wood on the left. Continue in the same direction to Leeshall Farm to reach a lane.

3. Turn right onto the lane. When the road bends to the right, turn left onto a track. Follow the track around a right-hand bend to a lane. Turn right and in 20 metres turn left at a public footpath sign. The path bears to the left and drops downhill through trees to a private dwelling house. A track runs alongside the house, which is in a quite exceptional setting. At a T-junc-

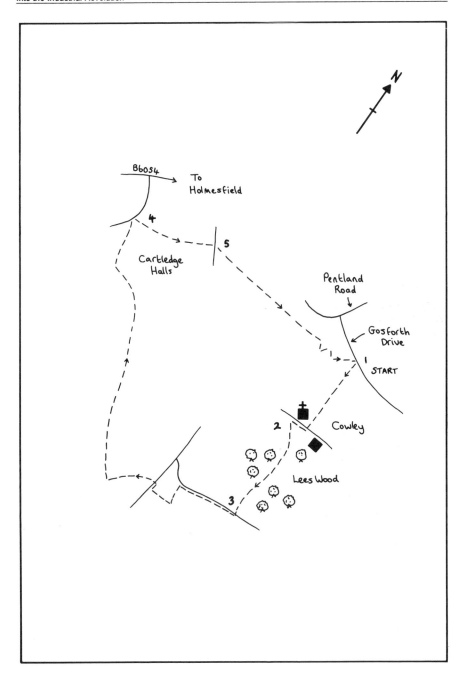

tion turn right onto a clear track, which eventually leads to the two Cartledge Halls.

It is thought that John Wolstenholme built the first hall in 1492. His grandson, also called John, married Catherine Fanshaw from nearby Fanshaw Gate. He was a founder of the Virginia Company and helped Henry Hudson launch his expedition to find the North West passage. Wolstenholme Island in Baffin Bay is named after him. John and Catherine had three sons. One of their sons, yet another John, was a Royalist officer in the civil war who was killed on his way to Marston Moor in 1644.

Cartledge Grange was built in the mid-16th century opposite Cartledge Hall and blocking the view of the original hall in what is thought to have been a fit of family spite of the Burton family who acquired Cartledge Hall by marriage in 1556. After the civil war the history of the Hall remains unknown, but it became a farmhouse at some stage.

The hall came into the ownership of the Lucas family at the end of the 19th century and was tenanted by the novelist Robert Murray Gilchrist. Robert died in 1917 and by the time his sister passed away in 1947 the property was in a poor state of repair. Basil Doncaster then purchased the property and restored it to its current condition.

4. Shortly after the two halls the route reaches a T-junction. Turn right over a stile signposted for Cowley Bar. Initially the path follows the field edge before swinging to the left across the field to a gate. Go through the gate and follow the field edge to a stile. Climb the stile and turn left onto a track. Just before reaching a lane a yellow waymarker points the route through a gate on the left. Walk along the field edge to a stile. Climb the stile and cross over the lane to join a bridleway.

5. The bridleway leads into a wooded area. Keep along the right-hand edge of the wood to emerge from the trees by a small farmhouse. The track then returns you to the housing of the Gosforth Valley. Turn right on reaching the road. The road bends first to the left, then to the right and back to the left again. Turn right at the T-junction and return to the starting point.

Trail 20 – Millthorpe

Distance: 8 kilometres/5 miles

Start: The bottom of Millthorpe Lane (small parking area) at the junction with the B6051 at Millthorpe near the Royal Oak public house

Maps: OS Outdoor Leisure 24 The Peak District White Peak Area

Refreshments: The Royal Oak public house at Millthorpe

Toilets: None

Key Features: Very extensive views in all directions

Route Instructions

1. Cross over the junction with the B6051 and take the public bridleway called Mill Lane opposite.

The Royal Oak stands to the right of this junction. Up until the 1930s a bakestone stood here where oatcakes were made from meal ground at the mill.

At the ford with Millthorpe Brook use the footbridge provided.

Until 1971 when it was demolished, there was a corn mill near the ford.

On reaching the entrance to Mill Farm ignore the stile in the wall and take the path hedged on both sides to the left of it. It is usual to have to leave this ancient hollow way for a short while on reaching a stream. Cross the footbridge if the stream is impassable and climb a stile on the left into a field. Turn right to walk alongside the hollow way and rejoin the original path on reaching a gate. Follow this path to a lane at Johnnygate.

2. Cross over the lane and walk along the left-hand edge of a field heading towards Broadmeadow Wood. Climb a stile into the woodland and follow the path, which bears to the right, crosses a brook and leaves the woodland by a stile at a corner. Follow a field edge with the wood on your right for 50 metres before joining a track. The track follows the left-hand edge of two fields. In the next field the track forks. Bear to the left and head up through gorse bushes first round to the right and then to the left up to a farm. Pass through the farm onto Far Lane at the small settlement of Rumbling Street.

3. Cross over the lane and climb a stile in a wall. Walk along a field edge with the hedge on the left. Crowhole Reservoir is over to the right. Climb a stile and continue in the same direction dropping downhill to Crowhole Brook. Close to the bottom bear to the right to cross the brook and head steeply uphill at the other side for 20 metres to a stile by a public footpath sign next to a large holly bush. Climb the stile onto a lane and turn right. In 15 metres climb another stile on the left by a public footpath sign. Walk uphill with a wall on the left and then across the middle of a field, passing a telegraph pole, and up towards a stile at the top of the field. If you turn around at this point there are magnificent views of Holmesfield along the ridge top in front of you, the Peak District to the left and Sheffield over to the right. In the next field walk along the left-hand edge of the field and follow it round to the right on reaching the corner. In 20 metres, turn left through a gap in between two gates. Follow a field edge to a stile at the side of a building. Climb the stile onto Grange Lane.

4. Turn right onto the lane.

Along this lane there are views over to the left of Chesterfield and its crooked spire and Bolsover Castle can also be seen on the ridge top in the distance.

Opposite to a T-junction, turn right over a stile by a public footpath sign. Follow a field edge with the wall on the right initially. Later the path passes in between two walls for a short while and then the wall is only on the left. Climb a stile at the side of a gate and follow a field edge to another stile. Climb the stile and follow a faint path to the right across the middle of a field heading for a gap in large holly hedge. In the next field a farm can be seen over to the right. Continue in the same direction to a stile at the other side. Climb the stile and cross a track in the middle of the field making for Grange Wood in front of you. Drop steeply down through the trees to a footbridge and back up the other side to a stile. Keep straight ahead across the middle of a field to a gap in a wall and onto a stile at the other side of the next field. Climb the stile and look out for a white gate, which leads the way back onto Far Lane.

5. Cross over the lane and join the sign posted public right of way. This clear track eventually leads into Hollin Wood. At the other side of the wood, 75 metres before the track becomes a surfaced lane, a path crosses the track. Turn left through a gap in the wall and drop steeply down to cross a brook. Bear over to the right across a field to a small stile. On crossing this stile you are in a field corner. Follow the field edge with the hedge on the left and in the next field walk across the middle of the field into Rose Wood. Continue in the same direction through the woodland dropping

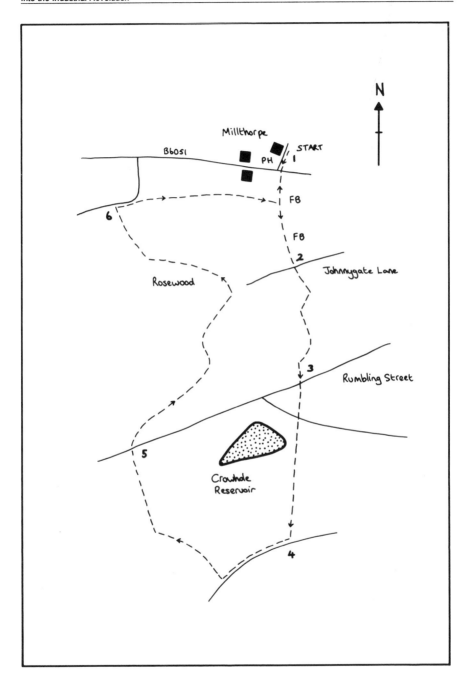

down to a footbridge over Pingle Dike. Seventy-five metres further on the path reaches an edge of the wood. Leave the woodland path and turn right though a gap in the fence into a field with a farm in front of you. Walk across the middle of a field. Pass through a gate onto a track, which runs along a field edge with a hedge on the right. Climb a stile and make for another stile by a public footpath sign at the other side in between a house and a bungalow.

6. Turn right onto a lane. When the lane bends to the left in 75 metres continue straight ahead at a public footpath sign along a field edge. Climb a stile and follow the ridge with Millthorpe Brook on the left. After the next stile the path leads back to Mill Lane where you turn left and return back over the ford and to the starting point.

Trail 21 – Holymoorside and The Hipper Valley

Distance: 6.5 kilometres/4 miles

Start: Road side parking at Holymoorside next to the Bull's Head in between the playing field and the River Hipper

Maps: OS Explorer 269 Chesterfield and Alfreton; OS Outdoor Leisure 24 The Peak District White Peak Area

Refreshments: Public houses at Holymoorside

Toilets: Holymoorside

Key Features: The village of Holymoorside and the all-round views on a clear day

---

The large village of Holymoorside lies in the valley of the River Hipper and is surrounded by beautiful countryside.

Route Instructions

1. Walk to the road junction where the Bull's Head is situated and cross over onto Loads Road. After 50 metres bear left at a junction by the Lamb Inn. The road heads uphill. Continue straight ahead at the crossroads. 200 metres past the crossroads there is a footpath sign on the left near a National Speed Limit sign. Turn left and walk uphill on a track walled on the right and fenced on the left. The track eventually bends to the right and follows the edge of a ridge before beginning to drop downhill. Virtually at the bottom of the hill cross a stream and then bear left at a fork and drop down onto a lane.

2. Turn right and then left in 50 metres at a public footpath sign onto a track. Cross a footbridge and continue through the woodland to a stile and later by a wall on the left. The path leaves the woodland and reaches a gate in front of Stonehay Farm. Pick up the gravel track, which bends to the left in front of the farm. This clear track leads to the B5057.

From here the tall chimney built in 1770 of the old "Pig of Lead" smelting site can be seen. Stone Edge Cupola is a listed ancient monument and is the most important and best-preserved lead-smelting site in Derbyshire. It is also quoted in the Guiness Book of Records as the oldest freestanding

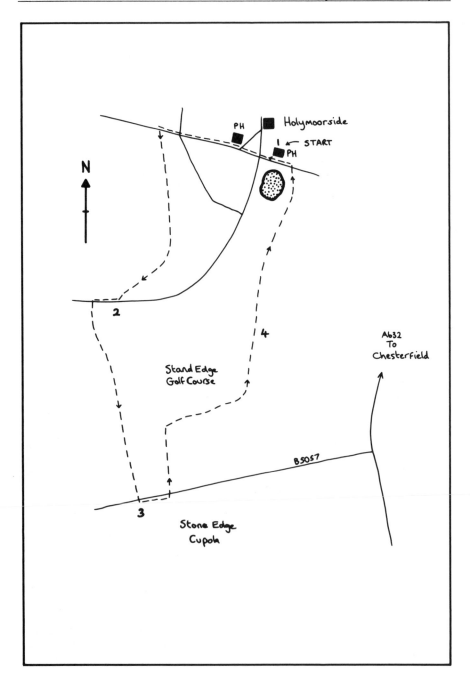

Stone Edge Cupola

industrial chimney in Britain. If you wish to visit the site, applications should be made to Spitewinter Farm. Cupolas replaced boles, hence the name frequently seen in North-East Derbyshire of bolehill, (ore hearth). They were used for the smelting of lead and were always located on exposed hilltops.

3. Turn left and left again in 100 metres at the public footpath sign onto the access road to Standedge Golf Club. The lane bends sharply to the right and then leads past the Golf Club House. When the lane bends to the left continue ahead to a stile. Climb the stile and cross a fairway with care. Please respect the players. At the other side of the fairway turn left by a wall and public footpath sign to walk initially with the wall on your right. Continue to follow the edge of the golf course until you are virtually opposite a green. Here look out for a public footpath sign on your right.

4. Turn right into woodland. At a fork keep right and shortly afterwards join a track walled on both sides, which drops downhill along the edge of Gladwin Wood. Virtually at the bottom of the hill pass through a gap in a wall and walk down to a track in 30 metres. Turn right onto the track and follow it to Woodside Farm. In front of the farm leave the track and bear half left onto a grassy path for 100 metres before crossing a stream and entering woodland. Climb a stile and at the fork keep left along the edge of the wood. Climb another stile and pass the dam on your left. On reaching a lane in Holymoorside turn left and return to your starting point.

Trail 22 – Walton

Distance: 7.3 kilometres/4½ miles

Start: Roadside parking on Foljambe Avenue off Matlock Road at Walton by The Blue Stoops public house

Map: OS Explorer 269 Chesterfield and Alfreton

Refreshments: The Blue Stoops and The White Hart on Matlock Road

Toilets: None

Key Features: The Great Pond of Stubbing and views over the Hipper and Rother valleys

Route Instructions

1. From The Blue Stoops cross over Matlock Road and take the public foot-path opposite with houses on the right and woodland on the left. In 100 metres turn right onto a path which is, initially, fenced on both sides. The path emerges onto Chesterfield golf course. Turn right and walk with the golf course on your left for 200 metres to a corner. At the corner enter woodland and cross two footbridges in quick succession. The path then passes over a section of the golf course before crossing another foot-bridge and entering Walton Wood.

2. The track through Walton wood is clear and wide. Keep straight ahead at a crossroad of tracks. At the other side of the wood turn right onto a path that runs along an edge of the wood and a wire fence on the left. Follow the wire fence until a T-junction with a wide track is reached. Turn left at the T-junction and soon emerge from the wood by a gate. Continue along the edge of a field on a track to Matlock Road. The White Hart public house is on the right. Turn left onto Matlock Road and cross over the road to walk gently uphill on the pavement. 20 metres before the driveway to Broadgorse Farm turn left at a public footpath sign.

3. The path soon leads to the driveway for the farm. At the fork bear right and walk up towards the farmhouse. Just before a gate look out for a stile in the wall. Climb the stile into a field and turn left to walk with the farm buildings on the left to a stile in the field corner. After the stile the path veers to the left and crosses a stone footbridge over a stream. Climb a stile on the left in 10 metres and turn right to walk uphill along a field edge

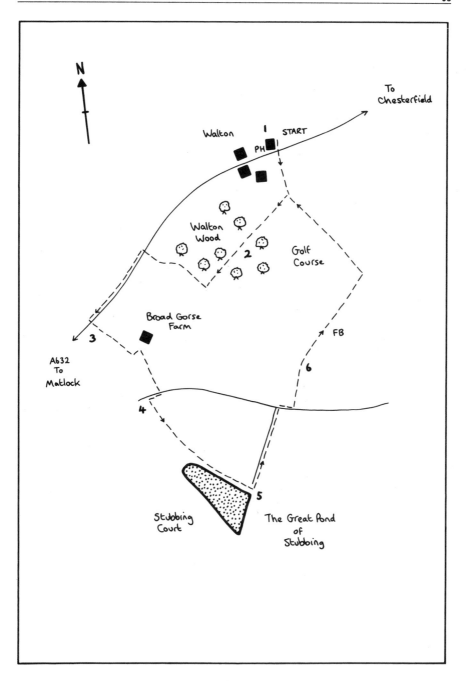

The Great Pond of Stubbing

with the hedge on the right. Walk alongside farm buildings to a stile in the far right-hand corner of the field.

4. Climb the stile onto a lane. Turn right and walk past the entrance to Harperhill House Farm and in 50 metres turn left at a public footpath sign. Walk along a track in between houses. On reaching the end of a line of trees turn left to walk along the top of a ridge in between the trees. At the end of the trees climb a stile and continue in the same direction. The Great Pond of Stubbing is on the right and Stubbing Court is further over to the right beyond the pond.

The house at Stubbing Court was built in the early 18th century. In the 1880s Harold Soames the father of Olive Baden-Powell bought Brampton Brewery and moved his family into Stubbin Court. Olive was born here in 1889 and went onto become the founder of the Girl Guide Movement. Her husband, Lord Baden Powell is probably better known as the founder of the Boy Scout Movement.

5. At the end of the pond climb another stile onto a lane. Turn left and then right at a T-junction. In 20 metres turn left over a stile at a public footpath sign for Boythorpe. Walk along a field edge with the hedge on the right to a stile. Continue ahead and in 50 metres climb a stile on the right. Walk along a field edge again with the hedge on the right to another stile. Climb the stile and walk to the left along a path in between woodland on the left and houses on the right. At the end of the housing the route emerges onto a playing field. Walk across the middle of the playing field to enter Walton Wood by two upright stones. The path bears to the right in the wood. Keep on the main track. In 200 metres, cross a footbridge on the edge of the wood.

6. Walk across the middle of a field to a footbridge over Birdholme Brook. After the footbridge bear to the right for 20 metres and then turn left to walk uphill with the Chesterfield golf course on the left. At a fork keep to the right. Just before the brow of the hill the path meets a track. Turn left and walk downhill and into woodland. The path runs in between a line of trees and leads to the car park for the golf club house. Rejoin the woodland path ahead for a short while before reaching the surfaced driveway to the clubhouse. Here leave the woodland and join a gravel track with houses on the left. This track runs back to Matlock Road by The Blue Stoops. Cross back over the road and return to the starting point.

Trail 23 – Rother Valley Country Park

Distance: 10.5 kilometres/6½ miles

Start: Bedgreave Mill Visitor Centre Car Park in Rother Valley Country Park. The entrance to the park is on the A618, between Killamarsh and Wales Bar.

Map: OS Pathfinder 744 (SK48/58) Aughton & Carlton in Lindrick

Refreshments: Visitor Centre and public houses in Killamarsh

Toilets: Visitor Centre

Key Features: Rother Valley Country Park, Bedgreave Mill, a section of the Trans Pennine Trail and a section of the Chesterfield Canal.

Route Instructions

1. From the car park walk to the Rother Valley Lake and turn right to join the lakeside path. Follow the lake as it bends to the left and passes an adventure playground on the right. The path runs in between Rother Valley Lake and the Northern Lake. At a T-junction turn left and pass through a gate in 50 metres. The broad lake side track leads to another gate. After passing through this gate turn right to leave the park.

2. Shortly after passing under a railway bridge turn left at a public footpath sign to join the Trans Pennine Trial. Follow this as it crosses over the B6058. Continue ahead until you are opposite a new housing area over to the right. In between the trail and the housing the River Rother can be seen. Just past the new housing there is a crossroads of paths. Turn left and double back on yourself to cross a stile.

3. The path crosses over the Chesterfield Canal frequented by fishermen, and heads uphill to a footbridge over a disused railway. Cross the bridge and continue gently uphill, along the edge of a field with the fence on your right. At a crossroads continue ahead on a surfaced path in between houses. On reaching a road, cross over and join the path on the other side still running through housing. The surfaced path then changes to a rough path, which leads to garages. Bear left to a road. Cross over and then turn left onto Rectory Road. Where this road bends to the left, turn right along a path, which leads to The Blacksmiths Arms.

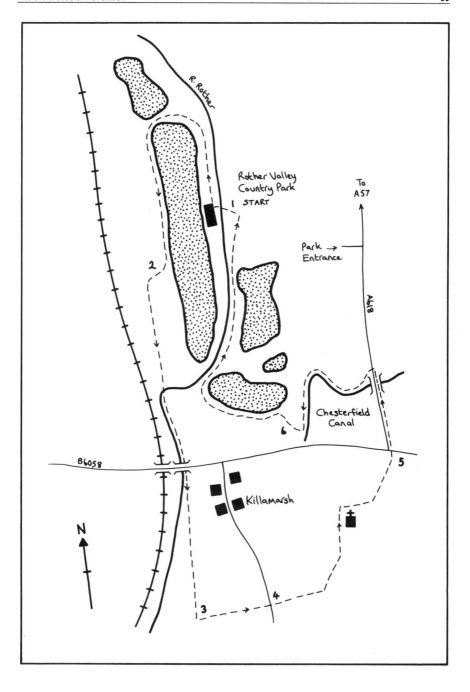

4. Cross over and head up the lane to the left-hand side of the public house. After 10 metres turn right at a public footpath sign. This path leaves the housing area and joins a sports field. Turn left onto the field and walk downhill to the end of the field. The path off the field is close to the far left-hand corner of the field and to the left of the marker post in the middle of the field. The path drops down some steps and continues downhill. At a fork in 50 metres, keep left over a stile. The path follows the edge of a field with a hedge on the right to a stile. On reaching a lane continue ahead and turn right immediately after The Crown onto Church Lane. The church is on your left. When the lane bends sharply to the right, turn left just after the last house onto a surfaced path, which runs along the edge of a playing field.

5. Cross over the B6058 and turn left at the roundabout onto Rotherham Road. Just before the Angel Inn join the Chesterfield Canal on your left at a stile. This section of the canal can become overgrown in the summer. Cross another stile after 75 metres and turn left. Keep left to rejoin the canal towpath in a few metres. The towpath bends to the right. Keep left at a T-junction of paths and ignore a marker post and path off to the right at the crown of the bend in the canal. The canal then bends back to the left. Just before reaching the end of a field and some houses there is a small path through the hedge to your right, which leaves the canal towpath and passes under the wire of a telegraph post. The path bends to the left and drops down onto a track.

6. Turn right and then immediately left at a yellow waymarker. The path leads to Nether Moor Lake. Turn left to follow the edge of the lake with the lake on your right. Follow the lake edge passing football pitches on your left. In the corner of the football pitches start to move away from the lake to join a gravel track 50 metres from the lake. The track passes in between trees and joins the River Rother on your left. Meadowgate Lake is on your right. On reaching the main entrance road to the park turn left. Follow the road to the left over a bridge and then right at a T-junction. The car park is on your left.

Trail 24 – Five Pits Trail to Sutton Scarsdale Hall

Distance: 14.5 kilometres/9 miles

Start: Grassmoor Country Park off Birkin Lane, Grassmoor

Map: OS Explorer 269 Chesterfield and Alfreton

Refreshments: The Elm Tree Inn at Heath

Toilets: None

Key Features: Grassmoor Country Park, a section of the Five Pits Trail, the village of Heath, and Sutton Scarsdale Hall

Route Instructions

1. From the car park facing the Park turn left as sign posted to the Five Pits Trail in 250 metres. Bear left at a junction under a bridge to join the trail. The path heads gently uphill to a junction of paths. Turn left and then right in 15 metres at a signpost for the "Five Pits Trail – Tibshelf" passing a pond on your left frequented by fishermen.

2. On reaching a road, cross over and continue ahead on the trail ignoring all side turnings and following the trail around several bends. Then after a relatively short straight stretch the trail splits. The route bears left as sign posted for the "Five Pits Trail – Holmewood" and then left again at the next two junctions in quick succession. On meeting a road rejoin the trail at the opposite side and follow it to the A6175 at Holmewood.

3. Cross over onto Devonshire Terrace, passing the Holmewood Hotel on your left. A little further on just before a right-hand bend, a surfaced path bears off to the left and drops down to a road. Cross over the road and take the path at the other side. Look out for the Five Pits Trail sign in 20 metres, which turns off to the left. You will now be walking with industrial units on your left and houses on your right. The trail starts to move further away from the houses, but when you are almost opposite the last of the houses at a T-junction of tracks with two posts on either side, turn right. The path takes you past houses on your right to a lane.

4. On the opposite side of the lane walk along a field edge with the hedge on your right to a stile. Climb this stile and another stile at the end of the next field. Now head for a stile in the middle of the far end of the next field. If you climb over this stile a path takes you to the road through the charming village of Heath.

Heath is recorded in the Domesday Book as two settlements, Lunt, on the site of the remains of the original 12th century church. This is now separated from the village by the A617. Le Hethe was to the west. They probably combined into one village in the 12th or 13th century. The village passed from Robert de Ferrars, the first Earl of Derby to the monks of Gerondon Abbey. After the Dissolution, it passed through several wealthy families. The village has two Grade II listed buildings, one being the remains of the church already mentioned and a thatched cottage at the northern end of the village.

5. Turn left and when the road bends to the left by the church cross over to a track on the other side.

There is a thatched cottage just before the bend and The Elm Tree Inn is 50 metres to the left of the bend. If you turn right at the church this will take you to the remains of the original church.

Climb a stile. The track drops down to a bridge over the A617. Immediately after the bridge, turn left. The track follows the edge of a field with the hedge on your left. After 150 metres the grassy track bends to the right by the side of a telegraph pole and heads across the middle of a field down to a stream. Cross over a footbridge and walk along a field edge with the hedge on your right and later a plantation.

6. In the field corner turn left onto a track and look out for a stile in 75 metres on your right-hand side. Climb the stile and bear half left to a stile near the far left-hand corner of the field. In the next field, bear slightly to the left to another stile and onto a track. Cross over the track and climb another stile. Walk along a field edge with the fence on your right.

Over to your left the ruined walls are the remnants of a mansion built by Bess of Hardwick.

After another stile you will enter Wrang Plantation. The path bears to the left and over a footbridge and then to the left again uphill to emerge from the woodland. Walk along the edge of a field with a hedge on your right to Shire Lane.

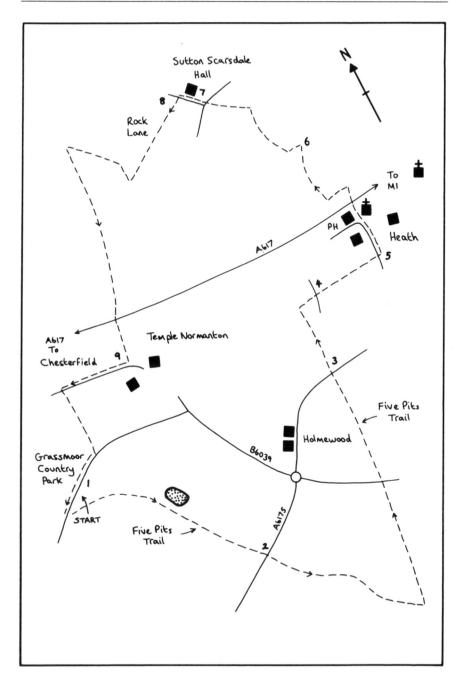

7. Turn right and follow the lane as it bends to the left into Sutton Scarsdale.

The parish of Sutton-cum-Duckmanton was formed in 1558 and life at that time centred on agriculture. From the 1790s the picture began to change with the building of the Adelphi Ironworks, which had two blast furnaces, a

Sutton Scarsdale Hall

foundry, brick works and collieries. Industrialisation received a further boost in the 1880s when the Arkwright family leased their rights to extract coal to the Staveley Coal and Iron Company, who built the nearby Arkwright Town.

Sutton Scarsdale Hall is signposted to the right by an information board.

The hall was once one of the most magnificent properties in Derbyshire, which is now in the hands of English Heritage. It was built in 1774 by Nicholas Leake, who was the fourth and last Earl of Scarsdale. Nicholas was once the Crown's Ambassador to the Holy Roman Empire, but as he allegedly plotted with the Jacobite rebels in 1715 he was sent to the Tower of London. He was later able to buy his freedom.

Nicholas inherited a Jacobean house on the present site, but had the architect Francis Smith design a more fashionable Baroque property around its nucleus.

In 1824 the Hall passed to descendants of the famous industrialist Richard Arkwright and it remained in his family until 1926. It was then purchased by a speculator, who sold everything that could be removed. The ruins were then saved the day before they were due to be pulled down by Sir Osbert Sitwell from Renishaw Hall after the Second World War. Sir Reresby Sitwell then passed the shell to the Ministry of the Environment.

50 metres past the information board turn left onto Rock Lane.

8. Rock Lane is a surfaced track to begin with. Ignore the first public footpath off to the left. At the second signpost, turn right to walk along a field edge with the hedge on your right. The path bends to the left and heads towards trees and a house. Just after passing through a band of trees there is a public footpath sign at a T-junction. Turn left onto a track, which heads gently downhill through woodland and a scattering of houses. On reaching a public footpath sign at a T-junction bear to the right and follow the track as it heads uphill and becomes a surfaced lane to pass under the A617.

9. At a T-junction turn right. Ignore the first left and after 200 metres climb a stile on your left just before another road junction to join a track hedged on both sides. The maturing Grassmoor Country Park can be seen over to your right. On meeting Birkin Lane, turn right and return to the car park.

Trail 25 – Five Pits Trail and Pilsley

Distance: 7.3 kilometres/4½ miles

Start: The Five Pits Trail Car Park on Back Lane at Tibshelf. Back Lane is a side road off High Street in between the Wheatsheaf public house and the church of St John The Baptist

Map: OS Explorer 269 Chesterfield and Alfreton

Refreshments: Tibshelf

Toilets: None

Key Features: A section of the Five Pits Trail

Route Instructions

1. From the car park, turn right onto the Five Pits Trail passing a house called Claremont on your left. The Trail reaches Hardstoft Road on the outskirts of Pilsley. Cross the road to rejoin the Trail and continue onto Locko Lane. Here turn left to leave the Trail and then bear left at the fork in 50 metres onto Green Lane, which is sign posted for Pilsley.

2. The lane climbs gently uphill and then flattens out. Watch out for a public footpath crossing the lane and climb a stile on the left. Head across a field to the end of a fence and a yellow waymarker sign. Walk along a field edge with the hedge on your right. At the end of the field, turn left. You then turn right at a fence corner and continue to a stile. Pass through a farmyard to meet a lane on a bend. Turn left onto Back Lane in Pilsley and follow it round to the right onto Slacks Lane. 75 metres further on turn left at a public footpath sign.

3. The path runs initially in between houses and passes the end of a cul-de-sac. Keep straight ahead onto a play area and walk by a fence on the left. Cross a bridge over a stream and follow the clear path with houses on the right and a field on the left. Turn left at the road and then right in 100 metres onto Rouse Street. At the end of the road climb a stile. This clearly waymarked path then continues in the same direction over a series of stiles crossing a farm track opposite Sitwell Grange and, later, Westwood Brook before rejoining the Five Pits Trail at Tibshelf. Turn right on meeting the trail and retrace your steps back to the car park.

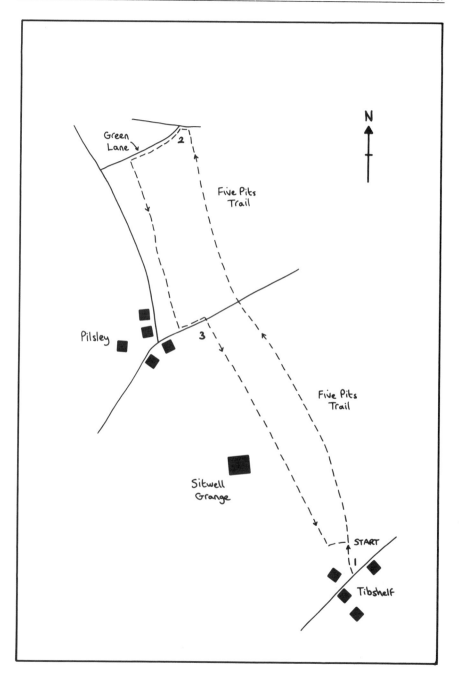

Trail 26 – Clowne

Distance: 9 kilometres/5½ miles

Start: The junction with Clowne Cross by the Anchor Inn, in the centre of Clowne. Take the road opposite the Anchor Inn. There is a car park 50 metres on the left next to Clowne District Office.

Map: OS Explorer 269 Chesterfield and Alfreton

Refreshments: Public houses at Clowne and Elmton

Toilets: None

Key Features: The village of Elmton and Clowne Linear Park.

Clowne is a town of some 7,500 people close to the border of Yorkshire and Nottinghamshire. It was occupied as a fort in Roman times; in more recent years, it became an important coal mining area. The original spelling of the village was 'Clune', meaning 'spring' – so Clowne probably takes its name from the number of springs in the area.

Route Instructions

1. Turn right out of the car park and right at the junction by the Clowne Cross. Then turn right again to walk past North Derbyshire Tertiary College. In 100 metres, as the road bends to the right, bear left to a metal gate and a Clowne Linear Park Information Board.

The Linear Park, which is in the ownership of Bolsover District Council was opened in 1992 on the site of the former Lancashire, Derbyshire & East Coast Railway. It was built in the late 1890s for coal collection from collieries along its route from Beighton to Langwith Junction. In 1907, it was taken over by Great Central Railway for passenger transport until the 1960s when it finally closed down. The limestone outcrop, which may have provided shelter for early man, known as Clowne Crags can be seen at the southern end of the park.

Follow the surfaced path as it bends to the right and passes through another metal gate. Keep straight ahead onto a rough track through the Park. At the end of the track drop down some steps onto a road.

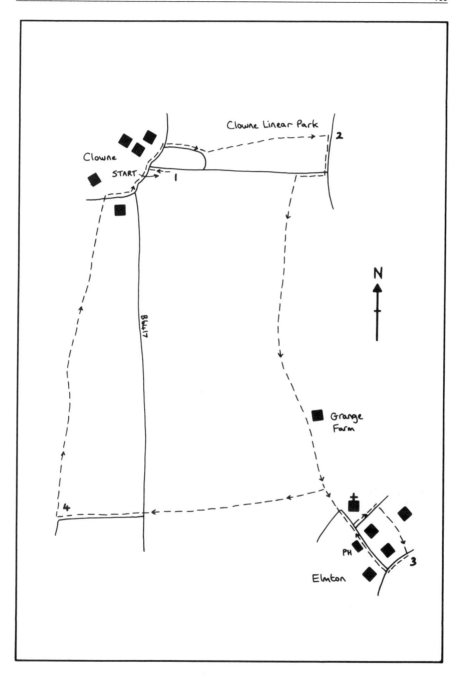

2. Turn right and walk uphill. The road bends to the right at a junction. 50 metres further on turn left onto a track virtually opposite Church Lane. Follow the track to a T-junction. Here turn left and keep left at the fork in 40 metres. Pass Grange Farm on the left and continue until you reach a lane. Turn left and left again just past St Peter's Church.

There has been a church on this site since Saxon times and it is mentioned in the Domesday Book. The church was largely rebuilt in the 18th century to a slightly unusual design.

When the road starts to bend to the left in 100 metres, turn right at a public footpath sign and walk along a field edge with the hedge on your right.

At the hedge corner head across the field at a slight diagonal to the left to another hedge corner. The path actually goes through the hedge corner. Turn right to walk with the hedge on your right. This quickly leads to a track and then onto a lane by the side of a house.

3. Turn right and follow the road as it bends to the right and into the village of Elmton with its many interesting cottages. On arriving back at the church continue ahead and back onto the track you left earlier for 75 metres before turning left onto Oxcroft Lane. At the T-junction, keep left. On reaching the B6417 cross over onto the lane opposite and follow this for 0.75 kilometres to a sharp left-hand bend.

4. Turn right at the public footpath sign and follow a field edge with the fence on the right to a stile. As you walk along the edge of a ridge continue across another two stiles in quick succession and head across the middle of a field to a stile. Climb the stile and cross a lane and over another a stile. Keep to the field edge with the hedge on your right and continue over a series of stiles along the ridge top. At the end of a playing field turn right over a stile. The path soon turns sharp left to join the B6418. Turn right and pass the White Hart on your left. Turn left at the T-junction and then turn right at Clowne Cross, which is possibly over 800 years old and marks a crossing of routes for travellers and return to the car park.

Transport Links

James Brindley's Chesterfield Canal

Canal construction began to boom around 1766 and the Chesterfield Canal was very much one of the first generation of canals to be built at the beginning of the Industrial Revolution. The impetus for this canal mania arose from the practical difficulties and expense to the business community of transporting heavy goods on a poor quality road network by packhorse or in carts. At that time bulk cargoes in North-East Derbyshire were transported by road to Bawtry, where they were transferred onto a boat, to be taken down the River Idle and then to the River Trent. The latter then provided easy access, in particular, to the rivers of eastern England, such as, the Thames.

Thus, the canal promoters, such as the London Lead Company, who were seeking a more efficient means of moving loads from their Ashover smelting mill to Hull, the Cavendishes who owned the furnaces and forge at Staveley and the coal barons of North-East Derbyshire, were all attempting to improve upon an existing trade route, rather than creating a new one. Under the guidance of the well-known canal engineer, James Brindley, the 46-mile length of water linking Chesterfield, Worksop and Retford through to the River Trent at West Stockwith, including 65 locks and two tunnels (Drakeholes and Norwood) was constructed between 1771 and 1777.

Brindley's plans were presented to the House of Commons and the Act of Parliament received Royal Ascent on 28 March 1771. Following James Brindley's death in September 1772 the project continued slowly due to considerable financial difficulties under the direction of one of his assistants called John Varley. The entire canal finally became operational on 4 June 1777, but within months, the ongoing problem of mining subsidence with the Norwood tunnel began.

The Chesterfield Canal was one of the first generation of canals at the cutting edge of technology. For its time it was a superb example of engineering boasting the longest tunnel in the country at Norwood and one of the earliest examples of staircase locks near Thorpe Salvin. The canal allowed the carriage of 20 tons plus of bulk cargo per load at "high speed" and provided substantial financial economies to industrialists. On the opening of the canal, the price of coal per ton at Retford dropped from 15s 6d to 10s 6d.

The financial problems and heavy borrowing during the construction phase meant that the canal was unable to make any trading profit until 1789. From then on through to the mid-19th century it remained relatively prosperous. Coal was the main cargo, but other bulk cargoes such as stone, lime, timber and iron were carried. Probably the most famous cargo was the stone carried from the Duke of Leeds quarry at Kiveton Park, which was used to rebuild the Houses of Parliament after a fire in 1834.

Once the canal became operational it soon became apparent that Pebley reservoir could not provide sufficient water storage facilities to meet the demand of the canal, therefore, reservoirs at Woodall and Killamarsh were built around 1790, followed by a further three at Harthill. The latter three reservoirs have now been combined into one.

Several branch canals, for example, the Adelphi, which linked the ironworks at Duckmanton were constructed, along with various tramways joining collieries and quarries to the canal. Various schemes were put forward to link the Chesterfield Canal into other inland waterways, but none of these proposals ever came to fruition. It was a combination of this isolation from the main canal network, the limited size of the working boats that were able to use it, the continuing difficulties with the Norwood tunnel and other mining subsidence problems between Staveley and Chesterfield, which contributed to the decline of the canal.

Additionally, like most canals the coming of the railways in the mid-19th century signalled the end of the canals future. To try and minimise the impact, the canal company formed its own railway and canal company. This combined company ultimately became part of the Great Central Railway.

Following another collapse of the Norwood tunnel in 1907 it was decided not to re-open the tunnel and the Derbyshire end of the canal was cut-off. By the 1950s, all commercial trading had ceased, but following extensive campaigning, the 26-mile length from West Stockwith to Worksop, which is in the hands of British Waterways, was made navigable for pleasure craft. The remaining 20-mile length from Worksop to Chesterfield is currently being restored for full navigation of the canal and work is progressing well under the impetus of The Chesterfield Canal Trust Ltd (previously known as The Chesterfield Canal Society), which was formed in 1976.

The working narrow boats that once plied the canal were all drawn by horse right to the very end of the working life of the canal and were known as Cuckoos. Unfortunately, no complete example of a Cuckoo is known to exist, but the canal towpath has been named The Cuckoo Way.

George Stephenson steams in

George Stephenson, and his equally gifted son Robert, have gone down in British history as two of the most outstanding civil engineers that this country has ever produced. George is popularly acclaimed as the "Father of the Railways" for his pioneering and significant contribution to the age of railway mania.

Stephenson was a colliery engineer in the North-East of England, who was responsible for the world's first public steam locomotive called "Locomotion" on the new Stockton and Darlington Railway in 1825. In 1830 George and his son Robert won the prize for the best steam locomotive for the new Liverpool and Manchester line with their world famous "Rocket", which attained a speed of 29 mph.

Later in George Stephenson's life, the North-Eastern corner of Derbyshire was to benefit both from his railway engineering feats and the impact he was to have on the local economy by exploiting previously undiscovered rich seams of coal and iron ore. In 1835, George visited the area looking for a suitable route to take trains from Leeds to Derby. Two years later, he started work on the North Midland Railway and this route was to pass under what at the time was the village of Clay Cross. This double track tunnel, which passes directly beneath Clay Cross, required 15 million bricks, it went down to a depth of 144 feet and cost £105,460. The course of the tunnel can easily be traced on the surface by 9 airshafts and it is, of course, still very much in use today by the Inter City trains. As the tunnel is almost a mile long, it has become known locally as the "mile-long tunnel".

Whilst the navvies were digging the tunnel out massive deposits of coal and iron ore were discovered and in 1840 George Stephenson launched the Clay Cross Company to take commercial advantage of the mineral resources. The Company sank a number of deep pits in the area and had interests in limestone, quarrying, lime burning, iron, the making of coke and bricks as well as coal mining. In 1844, it became the first company to send coal to London entirely by train and this provided North-East Derbyshire with a valuable and cheap transport system to its markets, which led to a boom in coal mining and other commodities and consequent prosperity to the local economy. The growth of Clay Cross alone was phenomenal.

George Stephenson was to take up residence at Tapton House in Tapton during the building of the North-Midland Railway, but by this time of his life he had begun to pass the legacy of his business interests onto his son Robert. For example, Robert was to succeed him as the

Chairman of the Clay Cross Company. In his last few years George was enjoying agricultural and horticultural pursuits at Tapton House and his gardens were renowned for a very good icehouse. After his death in 1848, he was buried at Holy Trinity Church in Chesterfield town centre. Tapton House passed to the Markham family in 1872 and then to Chesterfield Borough Council in 1925. The Clay Cross Company still exists today as part of Biwater Industries Ltd.

Trail 27 – Tapton Lock

Distance: 9 kilometres/5½ miles

Start: Road side parking by the Chesterfield Canal and Tapton Lock Visitor Centre

Map: OS Explorer 269 Chesterfield and Alfreton

Refreshments: Tapton Lock Visitor Centre, public houses in Brimington and the clubhouse at Tapton Golf Course

Toilets: Tapton Lock Visitor Centre

Key Features: The Chesterfield Canal – a section of the Cuckoo Way and the Trans Pennine Trail and the Tapton Lock Visitor Centre

Route Instructions

1. With your back to the visitor centre turn left onto the Chesterfield Canal towpath, which signposts the River Trent 45 miles away, so that you are walking in between the canal on your right and the River Rother on your left. Pass under two railway bridges in quick succession and a Sainsburys supermarket on your right. Cross over the B6050 on the outskirts of Brimington and rejoin the towpath. The route soon passes Wheeldon Mill lock and crosses another road. Continue onto Bluebank lock and then onto Bilby Lane.

2. Turn right onto a footbridge to cross the canal and follow a clear track towards houses at Brimington. On reaching the houses and a road continue straight ahead. Turn left at a roundabout onto Devonshire Street and then right at the next junction by The Ark Tavern onto the A619. Cross the A619 with care and turn left onto Briar View just after St Michael's Nursing Home. Immediately bear to the right at the fork onto a rough track passing Ivy House Farm. Climb a stile in front of you leaving the residential area and dropping gently downhill to a stile. Climb the stile and continue downhill to a footbridge.

3. After the footbridge head half right across the middle of a field uphill to a corner of woodland. Follow the edge of the woodland for 20 metres and then bear to the left to follow a field edge on your left to a stile. Cross over the lane by Tapton Hall Farm and continue straight ahead with farm buildings on your right to another stile in 75 metres. Climb the stile and

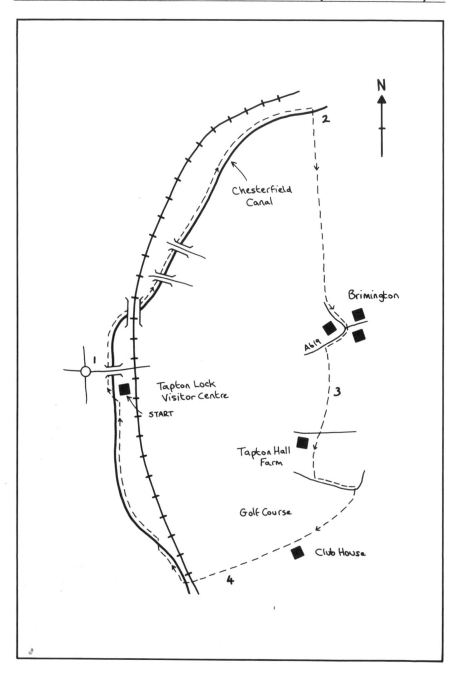

N

Chesterfield
Canal

2

Brimington

A619

1

Tapton Lock
Visitor Centre

START

3

Tapton Hall
Farm

Golf Course

Club House

4

keep straight ahead at a crossroad of tracks before reaching lane. Turn left onto the lane and walk with Tapton Golf Course on your right.

When the road bends sharply to the left turn right onto a bridleway. Follow the clear track with care across the golf course to the clubhouse. Here continue on the surfaced driveway of the club to a T-junction.

4. Turn right and follow the road as it bends to the right and passes under a railway bridge. Immediately after the railway bridge, turn right over a bridge across the River Rother. Turn left to walk with the river on your left to a road. Turn left, which takes you back over the river, and then turn right in 10 metres by a public footpath sign onto Holbeck Close. There is a Trebor Bassett building on the left. At the end of the road, a public footpath sign close to a Chesterfield Canal information board directs you back onto a path, so that you are walking with the River Rother on your right. In 200 metres turn right over a footbridge to walk on the other side of the river passing Arnold Laver on your right. The river and the Chesterfield Canal then split. The river goes off to the left and your route continues by the canal on the right. By the number 1 St Helana's lock cross over Tapton Mill Bridge to walk on the other side of the canal. The Tapton tunnel returns you to your starting point.

The Chesterfield Canal

Trail 28 – Kiveton and the Chesterfield Canal

Distance: 12.8 kilometres/8 miles

Start: Dog Kennel Hill – Kiveton Park Station – roadside parking on the B6059. Heading towards South Anston, pass the railway station on your right and the Station Hotel on your left. The road bends to the left. Park by the houses on your right.

Maps: OS Pathfinder 744 (SK48/58) Aughton & Carlton in Lindrick

Refreshments: Public Houses at Kiveton Park and Harthill

Toilets: None

Key Features: The Chesterfield Canal – a section of the Cuckoo Way and the village of Harthill

---

Route Instructions

1. Walk towards the railway station and opposite The Station Hotel turn left onto Manor Road. Cross the railway line and turn left onto the canal towpath at Dog Kennel Bridge, No 31.

This section of the canal from Kiveton Park to the hamlet of Turnerwood is regarded by many as the most attractive section of the canal and it is an area rich in limestone. The four mile stretch of canal between the Norwood Tunnel and the Thorpe Locks is known as the Summit Pound, as this is where the canal is at its highest. Just before the next bridge, Thorpe Bridge, at Peck Mill Bottoms are the remains of a railway transhipment wharf.

Pass under Devil's Hole Bridge and Pudding Dyke Bridge to reach the top of Thorpe locks.

This flight of locks contains 15 locks, including two treble and two double locks, in just over half a mile. The locks used to be a local tourist attraction known as the Giants Staircase.

From Thorpe Locks Bridge the canal leads to Turnerwood Bridge and the picturesque hamlet of Turnerwood.

Along the route you will have seen limestone quarries over to your left. The cottages at Turnerwood were built to serve the local quarry.

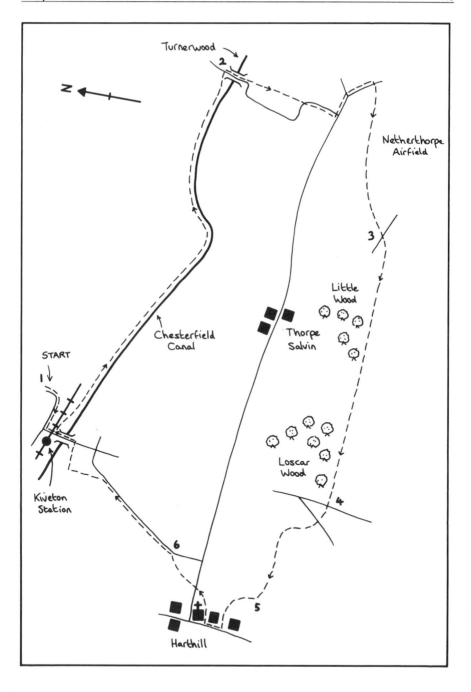

2. Leave the canal at Turnerwood Bridge and turn right over the bridge. The lane bends to the right by a telephone box. Just after the bend, turn left at a public footpath sign. The path heads across the middle of a field and rejoins the lane on a bend. Continue in the same direction to a T-junction. Turn left and then right in 50 metres by Brook House. At a public footpath sign by Top Farm, turn right. Head past the farm buildings to a small marker post and onto Netherthorpe Aerodrome. Keep to the fence on your right, which later becomes a hedge. In the field corner, there is another marker post. The path as marked on the map runs diagonally across the field to the far left-hand corner, where there is a public footpath sign. It may be easier to turn left and walk along the edge of the field to a lane. Turn right onto the lane and pass the public footpath sign referred to.

3. Just past Top Hall Farm on your right, turn left over a ladder stile by a public footpath sign. The path bears right and soon crosses a footbridge. Head through trees crossing two stiles and reaching a choice of three gates. Go through the middle gate in front of you. Continue in the same direction to another gate in the far right-hand corner of the field. Cross the middle of the next field to reach Southard's Lane. The path still continues in the same direction across a long field heading for a small marker post 20 metres to the left of a clump of trees known as Little Wood. Here continue for 100 metres to another marker post at a hedge corner. The path follows the hedge on your right. When the hedge ends continue across the middle of a field to a stile and public footpath sign on Packman Lane.

4. Climb the stile on the opposite side of the lane. The path cuts across a corner of the field to a stile, which is 50 metres over to your right. Climb the stile and follow the path half left to a stile and then onto another stile. The path then heads half right to a stile and public footpath, which leads onto Common Road. Turn left and in a few metres at the edge of a plantation turn right over a stile. Walk with the edge of the plantation on your right. At a T-junction of paths at the end of the plantation, turn left to walk along a field edge with the hedge on your right. Climb two stiles in quick succession by a line of trees and keep walking in the same direction across the middle of a field to a stile. Climb the stile and turn right and then left in the field corner. Follow the field edge with a hedge on your right to a stile. Follow the path across fields to a road in the village of Harthill.

5. Turn right onto the road, which bends to the left before reaching a T-junction. Turn right onto Union Street. Just after a World War 1 memorial and before the All Hallows parish church turn right onto a rough track. The

Turnerwood, Chesterfield Canal

track leads to the end of a cul-de-sac with modern housing. Follow the road to a T-junction. Turn right and after 10 metres leave the road by a public footpath sign on your left. The path follows housing on your left. At a T- junction turn right at a public footpath sign and head across the field to a stile. Climb the stile and head for a gate in the far left-hand corner of the field.

6. Turn left onto Manor Road. Follow this lane around a sharp left-hand bend and past Unsco Steels on your left. Just after the entrance to Unsco Steels there is a public footpath sign on your left. Walk down some steps onto a sports field and head along the edge of the field to a track. Turn right onto the track and follow it to a gate. Go through the gate and turn left onto a lane. Re-cross the railway line and turn right at the T-junction in front of The Station Hotel.

Trail 29 – Tapton Park

Distance: 9 kilometres/5½ miles

Start: Roadside parking on Manor Road by the junction with Westwood Lane. Manor Road leads from Brimington into Calow

Map: OS Explorer 269 Chesterfield and Alfreton

Refreshments: The clubhouse at Tapton Golf Course

Toilets: None

Key Features: Tapton Park and House, Westwood and The Openholes

Route Instructions

1. Start at Westwood Lane, which leads to Lodge Close, next to Special Effects hairdressers. At the end of Westwood Lane, continue straight ahead on the public bridleway by Lodge Farm. The path enters West Wood.

This is an ancient woodland at least 400 years old. Chesterfield Council now own the wood and are currently seeking to redress some of the neglect the wood has suffered in the last 100 years to provide a wildlife habitat. There are many collapsed sites of bell pits where early mining for coal and ironstone took place.

At a fork, turn right and cross a footbridge over Trough Brook. Bear left at a fork and then in 100 metres at a crossroad of paths turn left. Keep right at a T-junction and follow the yellow marker post ahead. At a junction of paths, turn left as indicated by the yellow marker post to drop steeply downhill to a footbridge.

2. After the footbridge bear to the right to a pond in 50 metres. Follow the edge of the pond round to some steps. At the top of the steps, walk along the Openholes, which is an important wildlife area.

The Openholes was littered with ironstone bell pits by 1600 and pits may have been dug here as early as the thirteenth century. About 1860, the Brimington Moor Iron Company, based at what is now Furnace Farm, had 50 coke ovens, a blast furnace and an engine house for the production of cast iron goods.

Pass Furnace Farm over to your left and continue straight ahead. Climb a stile to leave the woodland behind and bear left at a fork. Cross another

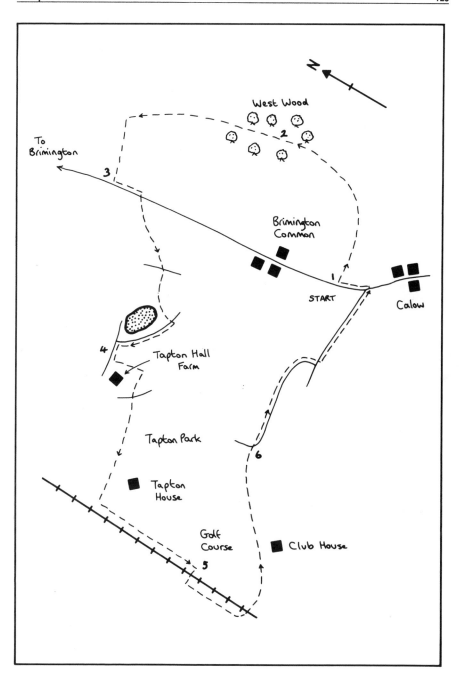

stile and then in 50 metres at a marker post turn left to climb another stile. Walk along a field edge with the hedge on your left to a stile. Continue in the same direction and over another stile before reaching a road on the edge of Brimington.

3. Cross over the road and turn left. Just after the Brimington Equestrian Centre turn right at a public footpath sign. At the end of the housing, the path bears half left across the middle of a field heading for the end of a line of trees. Pass through the trees to walk along a field edge with the hedge on your right to a track by some houses. Turn left and then right in 15 metres onto a bridleway. Walk in between a wall on the right and a wire fence on the left and follow the path as it drops down to a lane. Turn right and walk past a pond used by Chesterfield Angling Club. At the end of the pond turn left at a T-junction. Just before Tapton Hall Farm turn left over a stile by a public footpath sign.

4. Walk past farm buildings on the right and climb a stile in 75 metres. Continue along a field edge to a crossroad of tracks, which is by a marker post at the corner of woodland. A right turn here quickly brings you to a lane. Cross over the lane into Tapton Park and turn right to walk along an edge of the park to a marker post by a garden corner. The games court is over to the left. Keep in the same direction walking with housing on the right. Tapton House comes into view over to the left. The path bears to the left at the end of the housing and drops down to a children's play area. Take the track to the right-hand side of the play area, which moves closer to Stephenson's railway line and provides "inspiring" views of Chesterfield's crooked spire. The track, with Tapton Golf Course to the left, leads to a footbridge over the railway line.

5. Cross the footbridge and turn left onto a road. In 150 metres, just before a bridge over the River Rother, turn left to walk with the river on the right for 100 metres before turning right across a bridge. Turn left onto a road and pass under a railway bridge. Follow the road back over the River Rother and round to the left. At a right-hand bend turn left onto the driveway for Tapton Park Golf Club. In front of the Club House bear left at a "No Entry" sign for motor vehicles and onto a rough track, which leads across the golf course. Please take care whilst crossing the golf course and respect the players. At first the path drops downhill. At a marker post the tree-lined path then climbs back uphill to join a lane on a bend.

6. Continue straight ahead on Wheathill Lane and follow it around a right-hand bend onto Dark Lane. The road bends to the right again and leads to a T-junction. Turn left onto Westmoor Road, which takes you back to the houses of Calow. Turn left at the T-junction back onto Manor Road and return to the starting point.

Trail 30 – Clay Cross

Distance: 6.5 kilometres/4 miles

Start: Roadside parking in Clay Cross next to a small playing field by the junction with Windermere Road and the start of one end of the Clay Cross Tunnel. Approaching Clay Cross along the A61 (the Roman Ryknild Street) from Chesterfield pass the Church of St Bartholomew on the right and turn right at the junction with the George and Dragon public house

Map: OS Explorer 269 Chesterfield and Alfreton

Refreshments: Public houses in Clay Cross

Toilets: None

Key Features: Clay Cross Church, George Stephenson's railway line and a section of the South Chesterfield Way

---

Route Instructions

1. Walk back up towards Clay Cross and its church passing Mill Lane on the right. 100 metres further on turn left at a public footpath sign. Pass in between trees before emerging onto open land with the church of St Bartholomew standing prominently on the right.

Clay Cross rapidly expanded following the arrival of George Stephenson and his Clay Cross Company. At that time, the nearest church was at North Wingfield and this could not meet the requirements of the growing town. Not only did the Clay Cross Company provide the site for the church it also engaged the architect Henry Stevens. The Gothic style church was erected in 1851 with further additions over time.

Take the path that bears half left and passes through a gap in a hedge. 50 metres further on go through another gap in a hedge and follow the path round to the right soon reaching a footbridge by a pond, which is popular with fishermen.

2. Cross over the footbridge and turn left onto the South Chesterfield Way. This path which is hedged on both sides meets a track. Turn left onto the track and look out for a stile in 100 metres on the right. Climb the stile to walk with a field edge on your left to a stile. In the next field, head across the middle of the field and pass through a gap by the side of a gate onto a lane. Turn right and in 75 metres turn left at a public footpath sign. Pass

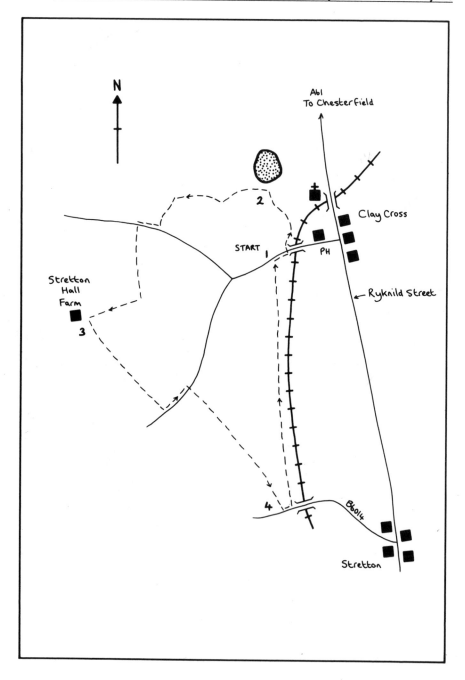

N

A61
To Chesterfield

2

Clay Cross

START 1

PH

Ryknild Street

Stretton
Hall
Farm

3

4

B6014

Stretton

by the side of a house named Greenacres into a field. Head across the middle of the field and through a gap in the hedge at the other side. Immediately turn right and climb a stile in the field corner. Continue in the same direction heading for Stretton Hall Farm first dropping down and passing through a gap in a hedge before gently climbing back up to the farm by a gate. Go through the gate and turn left in front of the farmhouse to leave the South Chesterfield Way.

3. Pass through another gate to leave the farm and head across the field to the far left-hand corner. Go through a gate and turn right to walk along a field edge with the hedge on the right. At the end of the field and after negotiating yet another gate bear left onto a track. The track passes Handley Lodge Farm. Continue ahead on the farms surfaced driveway to a lane. Turn left onto the lane and then right by a stream at a public bridleway signpost. Follow this clear path with the stream on the left to the B6014.

4. Turn left and then left again in a few metres through a black gate next to a house. The path runs alongside Stephenson's railway line on the right. Climb two stiles before emerging into a field. Continue in the same direction along the right-hand side of the field to another stile. In the next field, the path runs along the left-hand edge of the field and over a stile at the other end. On reaching the housing of Clay Cross, bear to the right to walk past a bungalow on the left and heading towards the church. The path returns you to the starting point.

Also of interest:

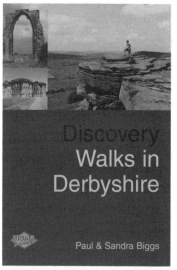

DISCOVERY WALKS IN DERBYSHIRE
Paul & Sandra Biggs
"This book promises an insight into some of the county's least known attractions and curiosities" THE LOUGHBOROUGH ECHO
£6.95

BEST PUB WALKS IN DERBYSHIRE
Martin Smith
Local ecologist, historian and Real Ale expert Martin Smith is uniquely qualified to write this guidebook!
£6.95

WALKING PEAKLAND TRACKWAYS
Mike Cresswell
"25 super walks written with style and wit" DERBY JOURNAL.
£7.95

DERBYSHIRE WALKS WITH CHILDREN
William Parke
"This must surely be the most complete walk book ever". DERBY EVENING TELEGRAPH
£6.95

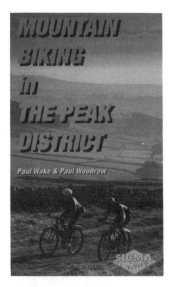
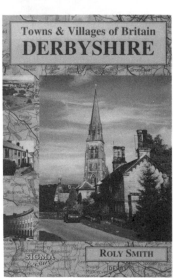